Developing your Business through Investors in People

NORRIE GILLILAND

Illustrated by Chris Tyler

Consultant Editor George Webster
Additional Research by George Meikle

Gower

Published by
Gower Publishing Limited
Gower House
Croft Road
Aldershot
Hampshire GU11 3HR
England

Gower
Old Post Road
Brookfield
Vermont 05036
USA

Norrie Gilliland has asserted his right under the Copyright, Designs and Patents Act 1988 to be identified as the author of this work.

British Library Cataloguing in Publication Data
Gilliland, Norrie
   Developing Your Business Through
   Investors in People
   I. Title II. Tyler, Chris
   658.312404

ISBN 0–566–07684–5

Library of Congress Cataloging–in–Publication Data
Gilliland, Norrie
   Developing your business through investors in people / by Norrie Gilliland: illustrated by Chris Tyler:
      consultant editor George Webster.
        p. cm.
      Includes index.
      ISBN 0–566–07684–5
      1. Employees—Training of. 2. Job enrichment. I. Webster, George. II. Title.
   HF5549.5.T7G477 1996
   658.3′124—dc20   95–23339
                                                                                          CIP

The guidance given in this book is based on the author's experience of working in training and development in a wide range of organizations, and his understanding of the Investors in People standard. It represents the author's view alone, and is given in good faith. No responsibility can be accepted for the effects of any acts or omissions by any individual or organization as a result of this advice. The Investors in People standard will inevitably change over time, as will accepted standards of good and best practice in human resource development. It is in readers' own interests to take up-to-date advice and guidance from the sources mentioned within this book.

Typeset in Palatino by Bournemouth Colour Press and printed in Great Britain at the University Press, Cambridge

Contents

| 6 | **Action** | 71 |

List of Figures

Preface

One of the government's National Education and Training Targets (NETT) is the Investors in People target. This says that, by the year 2000, 50 per cent of UK organizations will be recognized as, or committed to, the Investors in People national standard. There is an equivalent target in Scotland under the banner 'Education and Training Targets for a Competitive Scotland'.

At the time of publication, the penetration level of Investors in People in UK organizations is well under 5 per cent. So we have something of a challenge. One Local Enterprise Company (LEC) estimated recently that the national target for Investors in People in its area translates into about 3000 organizations by the end of the century. This LEC has under 100 companies committed and a handful of recognitions. Only 2900 or so to go.

But this masks the real challenge facing Investors in People – the challenge of quality. I believe that there is a danger of Investors in People losing the quality image it has so far managed to achieve. This view was confirmed by the words of one LEC director I spoke to recently:

> Of course I might achieve my share of the national targets for commitments and recognitions, if I focused the bulk of my resources on Investors in People. But even if I did that – which I can not – what would it really achieve? If I churned out, say, ten commitments/recognitions a week, what would that tell the world about quality?

This book is concerned with reaching out for the national targets, while maintaining quality.

What are the LECs and the TECs doing about it?

As you might imagine, the LECs and TECs (Training and Enterprise Councils) are committing resources in a number of ways, including

The government target for Investors in People is 50 per cent of all organizations by the year 2000. Current penetration is less than 5 per cent.

'Right, folks, only another 45 per cent to go.'

contracting with consultants like myself to advise and assess organizations. Some are hiring Investors in People advisors on short-term contracts, while others leave it to their full-time training and business development executives, to spread the word about Investors in People.

Despite lacking resources with which to do this more effectively, most of the LECs and TECs have been quite successful in attracting organizations to Investors in People. Interest is growing, and the number of organizations seeking advice seems likely to grow exponentially over the next two to three years.

Therein lies another problem. Having steered organizations to the point of committing to Investors in People, many LECs and TECs find themselves constrained in the help they can give them to prepare for assessment.

The resource deficiency

There is an unquestionable deficiency in resources, right across the country, to help organizations prepare for Investors in People.

While acknowledging the growing expertise on Investors in People within the LECs and TECs, it is true to say that some staff are still unsure of how the standard should be applied in individual organizations – which is understandable given that they are unable to commit much time to working with them. This leads to reluctance to advise companies in detail, in case the advice rebounds on them.

One solution of course is to put a consultant to work with an organization for a short time, but this assumes that there are sufficient experienced and high quality consultants available. Consultants working in the Investors in People field come from a wide variety of backgrounds – from human resources, quality, production engineering, and so on. Some of this experience is, of course, highly relevant to the Investors in People approach. But these consultants often lack the deeper understanding of *strategic* human resource development which is essential to get the real business impact that Investors in People offers.

Existing guidance

There is some helpful guidance material available from Investors in People UK, Investors in People Scotland, and some of the LECs and TECs. But, of necessity, this has to work at a fairly general level.

One of the great strengths of Investors in People is that it sets out a standard, and it is for organizations to decide how to meet it. The official literature cannot afford to be prescriptive, because that might diminish the thinking processes involved. Thus it is the responsibility of organizations and their advisors to work out what the standard means and how they should reach it. That is fine, so long as sufficient expertise and time is available within the organization or its advisors.

But this is beyond the means of most organizations – even some larger ones, which are unlikely to be carrying much by way of spare management capacity. Text books abound on probably every aspect of human resource development, but few are truly accessible to the majority of busy people. Some of them are unwieldy, over-academic, and not well suited to the task.

Who this book is aimed at

This book is designed to help anyone wishing to improve his or her knowledge of Investors in People in a practical setting. It is intended for use by:

- Training and human resource development people in organizations of all sizes;
- Directors, managers and business owners;
- Investors in People 'champions' – the people who are often delegated the task of preparing the organization for assessment, once top management has committed to Investors in People;
- Investors in People steering groups, which some organizations – even quite small ones – find helpful to the preparatory process;
- Trades unionists, who need to be abreast of current training and development issues;
- Staff in all parts of the LECs and TECs, whether or not Investors in People is their raison d'être;
- Intermediary and influencing bodies, such as Chambers of Commerce, industry bodies, training and education establishments, enterprise agencies and trusts;
- And – last but not least – the growing army of fellow consultants.

I hope they find it useful.

Awareness, assessment, advice and action

This book provides a tool to help everyone involved in Investors in People to translate the national standard into working practice. The broad way in which the standard is expressed – its greatest strength – causes endless confusion and debate. In one sense, that is as it should be.

It is not my desire to replace these very necessary thought processes, but to facilitate and enhance them. I will do this by:

- Describing what the national standard means, in a way that most people can understand;
- Putting forward my view of what meets the standard;
- Sharing hints, tips and examples of how some organizations have done it;
- Highlighting some traps for the unwary;
- Defining what is essential to meet the standard plus approaches that go beyond it, which might be 'good' for developing the business and its people even further.

You will see that this is not a typical textbook. It is meant as a workbook, with the emphasis on self-assessment and taking positive steps to close gaps in your human resource development policies and practices.

Above all, *Developing your Business through Investors in People* is designed to help you take practical, cost-effective steps to improve your business through developing your people. Theory has little place here.

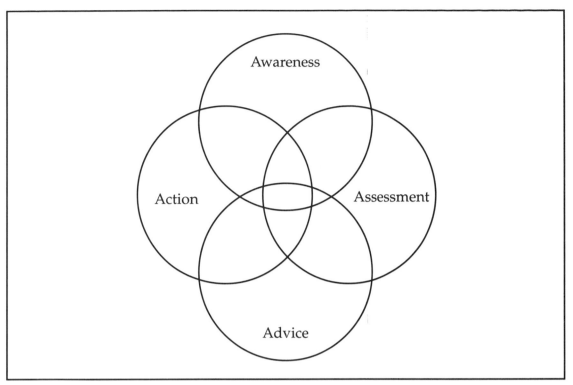

Figure 1   The four As

It is based on practical actions that organizations of various types and sizes have taken in order to improve.

So, I intend to:

● **Raise your Awareness** of Investors in People, clarify what it means, its true potential for business development, how the 24 Indicators can be applied to your business and how some other organizations have approached it;
● **Help you Assess** where you are in relation to the standard, and where you can improve;
● **Give Advice** where possible on how to do it; and
● **Enable you to take specific Actions** to move closer to the standard.

Figure 1 illustrates the interaction between these four 'As'.

Taking an eclectic approach

The book takes a rather eclectic approach; aspects of business and human resource development that may at first seem tangential to the main thrust of Investors in People are included because I believe they enrich the process. For example, when we look at individual contributions to the success of the business – encompassed by Indicator 1.5 – we need to ask what kind of contributions we expect people to make. Are you happy with a situation where people check in at nine and out at five and basically fulfil their job descriptions? Or are you looking for a bit of oomph?

The process will be enhanced, and your business will benefit all the more, by looking for ways to engage your workforce to the maximum – and therefore the book raises questions about gathering people's ideas, developing teamwork and opening up communications. You could become an Investor in People, I suppose, without ever getting one single idea from any of your employees – but that would be missing the point entirely. It would be a sterile approach to what could be the most powerful business development opportunity you have ever had.

If you cannot find one practical action or idea in this book to help you develop your business, write to me via my publisher telling me why, and I will personally refund your money.

If you are already convinced of the business benefits of Investors in People, and are aware of how it fits with other standards – such as BS5750 or ISO9000 – you might wish to skip the next few chapters and go right on to the practical applications, from Chapter 4 onwards. However, I suggest you consider the checklist opposite before you move on. It will give you a quick overview of how successful you are in achieving the best from your people. Ask them whether they agree with your answers. Or carry out the consultation exercise on pp. 8–9.

There are further details and checklists for each of the Investors in People Indicators in Chapters 4 to 7, each chapter dealing with the four Principles separately. Chapter 8 takes you through the preparation for Investors in People recognition and the assessment process itself.

Norrie Gilliland

Do *you* need Investors in People to develop your business?

	YES	NO
All our people kick into the same goal.	☐	☐
Our people would kill for this organization.	☐	☐
Our people bring us their best ideas.	☐	☐
Our reputation is good with the local community.	☐	☐
We use the 'inverted pyramid' approach to management.	☐	☐
There is a buzz about this place.	☐	☐
We accommodate our people's individual differences.	☐	☐
We really know what makes our people tick.	☐	☐
We almost always beat the competition.	☐	☐
We know where this organization is going.	☐	☐
We share that vision with our people.	☐	☐
Our customers like us.	☐	☐
Our bankers like us.	☐	☐
Our suppliers like us.	☐	☐
We are industry role models.	☐	☐

Acknowledgements

Many people contributed to the development of this book, notably those I have worked with in one way or another on Investors in People over the past few years, and from whom I have learned something new every day. They may find something of themselves in here. I hope what they now read will be a fair return for their knowledge and influence.

Special thanks for technical and moral support to Anne, Simon, Derek, and other friends at the David Hall Partnership.

NG

Introduction

The importance of setting Investors in People firmly in the context of business development cannot be overstated. Otherwise, it is in danger of being seen as 'just another government initiative'.

There is a need for practical advice, if we are to make a significant impact on the national target for Investors in People, and still retain quality within it. My main motivation for writing this book lies in my belief that Investors in People is potentially one of the most powerful business development models yet devised.

I have had direct experience of working with over fifty organizations of various shapes and sizes over the last couple of years, using Investors in People as a framework for developing their people in line with business objectives. During this time the potential for real gains became evident – but only if organizations use the Investors in People approach as a way of building new management cultures.

I have also seen the dangers of approaching Investors in People superficially. Needless to say, that is a complete waste of time, and very likely to rebound on the organization. Your people would spot it a mile away.

What's so different about Investors in People?

There is nothing new in Investors in People. But what differentiates it is the way it pulls various strands of business development and human resource development together for the first time, into a national framework.

Organizations involved in – or contemplating – quality initiatives, customer care programmes, and so on, will find Investors in People an ideal method for highlighting the training and development aspects of these approaches.

Blind ignorance and blind faith

Investors in People is not just concerned with training; understanding this is paramount. Too often, I have visited companies where managers know very little about training, and have a low regard for it. This, 'blind ignorance' is of course one of the key areas that Investors in People is trying to deal with. It is fundamentally important therefore to think much wider than training.

The flip side of the same coin is the 'blind faith' syndrome, which is usually expressed in the following terms – 'Training? oh yes, believe in it totally. Anyone who wants to go on a course gets it'. Frankly, this makes me cringe. On a recent visit to a small manufacturing company I was informed that the MD was very pro training. His concept of training was sending managers to business school (if they wanted it) or sending the engineer on a hydraulics course (if he wanted it). These may well have been relevant, but no attempt had been made to establish the business benefit of the training asked for. It was simply done because training was thought to be 'a good thing'. Meantime, there was no budget for developing the skills of the people on the production line.

Investors in People has, at long last, put training on the map. But we have to make sure it is properly targeted, delivered and evaluated.

It is an opportunity we simply must not miss.

The national standard

Investors in People is based on four Principles. The first part of the book describes these four Principles and some of the key issues involved in meeting them. The 24 Indicators are dealt with in detail in Chapters 4 to 7, which give advice on how to make them work best for your organization and examples of how other organizations have gone about it.

Please remember that the advice that follows is based on how I would approach the national standard. It is offered in good faith, but it is for you to decide what is most appropriate for your organization. There are no 'right' answers, no easy solutions. All I can offer is the benefit of my own experience.

Occasionally, I will suggest taking steps that go beyond the national standard. I will do so because I believe these approaches could add further value to your business, at little or no extra cost. Where I do go beyond the national standard, I will try to make this clear.

The Principles

The four Principles are:

1. **Commitment**
   An Investor in People makes a public commitment from the top to develop all employees to achieve its business objectives (see Chapter 4).
2. **Planning**
   An Investor in People regularly reviews the training and development needs of all employees (see Chapter 5).
3. **Action**
   An Investor in People takes action to train and develop individuals on recruitment and throughout their employment (see Chapter 6).
4. **Evaluation**
   An Investor in People evaluates the investment in training and development to assess achievement and improve future effectiveness (see Chapter 7).

It is useful to consider the four Principles in the context of what most organizations are trying to achieve – that is satisfied customers, committed employees, and financial returns (even in not-for-profit organizations).

The four Principles are best considered in a loop, as shown in Figure 2. Viewed in this way – within the context of satisfied customers, committed employees and financial returns – Investors in People can be recognized as a powerful business development tool, linking all training and development actions back to the organization's objectives.

Some key issues

The following are a few general but very important points about the four Principles and the standard itself. These are dealt with in greater detail under the relevant Indicators.

All employees

Principle 1 makes it clear that all employees should be covered by the organization's commitment, and its training and development activities. People often ask how literally this should be taken. My quick response to that is 'How much damage could that person do to your business?'

3

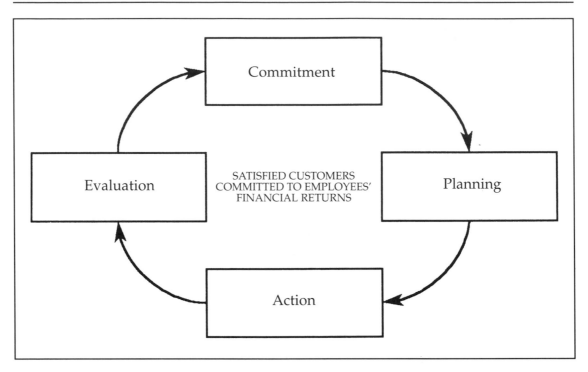

Figure 2   The Investors in People basic 'loop'. Investors in People links all training and development activities back to the business plan, in the context of achieving satisfied customers, committed employees, and financial returns.
Source: Ian Anderson/David Hall Partnership

- If a temporary secretary messes up an important communication and you lose an order, was that because you did not give that person sufficient information and support?
- If you run a residential home for elderly people, what about nurses who only work for you on occasions? Do you need to train and develop them? How much damage could these people do to your business, if you have not kept them up to date with developments in the company?
- If you brought in some temporary production workers to cope with a much welcomed rush order, would you need to explain to them how to do the job according to your quality standards? Could you afford not to?

Make sure also that:

- If you run a branch network, the furthest flung site is not neglected in training and development terms – and remember, that means communications too.

- If you use sub-contractors to deliver some of your core business activities, you consider carefully how you might include them in your communications and briefings. The more enlightened organizations would also include them in appropriate training sessions, because the successful delivery of their business depends on these associates.

So all people really means *all people*.

Real commitment from the top

Principle 1 also makes it clear that the commitment must come right from the top of the organization. That means the chief executive, managing director, chair, or equivalent, not one of the other directors – not even the personnel director. A token commitment will not suffice. This is as true for Investors in People assessors, who can detect tokenism at 100 paces, as it is for your own people – who are good at spotting it too. In many respects, they are the real assessors.

The importance of the line manager

Principle 2 places great emphasis on the role of the line manager – in fact this is a recurring theme throughout the standard. Unfortunately, it is one of the most neglected areas. Managers and supervisors are often the weakest link in the chain – and it is usually not their fault.

Time and time again I ask people how well their manager supports them in their training and development, only to be met with a blank stare. Investors in People simply cannot work without the active involvement of managers at all levels. But you have to support them in doing it. Don't fool yourself that managers will somehow just manage it.

Training and development options

The Investors in People standard is based on *training and development*. So recognize that training is just one aspect of development – in fact, I often feel there might be a case for outlawing the word 'training', because everybody thinks they know what it means, but few actually do. I prefer to use the word 'development', because human resource development can take many forms. Development involves engaging the talents and brains of your workforce. Training is only part of the equation.

Principles 2 and 3 in particular, are where the options for meeting training and development needs have to be understood. It is not simply a matter of sending people on training courses!

Evaluation

In Principle 4, the standard requires you to evaluate the effectiveness of your training and development actions. This is the area that tends to cause organizations most angst. Usually they are doing some kind of evaluation, but do not realize it.

If you employed sales staff, would you measure their sales performance on a daily, weekly, monthly basis? I bet you would. That sort of evaluation would give you a feel for whether the money you spent sending them on a sales training course last month was well spent. What did you hope to achieve for the business? What did it cost? Which of the staff have increased their sales since? What financial return have you achieved on your investment? What further help do individuals need to enable them to apply what they learned to the job?

Of course, it is not always that easy to evaluate the impact of training and development on the individual or the organization, but there are more possibilities than you might think. They just need to be brought to the surface – and refined or extended where necessary. You do want to know what bang you are getting for your buck, don't you?

You must provide evidence to show that you evaluate your training and development activities, to be recognized as an Investor in People.

Costs and benefits

A key element of Principle 4, which loops back to Principle 1, is that top management understand the costs and benefits of training and development. They must also show continuing commitment to developing people. That means training and development must be high on the management agenda. Management must embrace it – and visibly.

These key issues and how to deal with them in practical terms are discussed more fully within the relevant Indicators which follow.

The 'virtuous circle' of training and development

You may have come across the phrase 'virtuous circle of training and development'. Yes, it is a bit of a jaw-breaker, but when you flip it over, its importance becomes immediately apparent. Without it you would get a situation where people are not involved in the business, nobody gets any training, they continually make errors, and managers spend most of their time putting out fires. You may recognize this as the 'vicious circle', one with which so many organizations fight a daily battle. In fact, it is more invidious than that. It is a downward spiral from which many organizations are unable to escape.

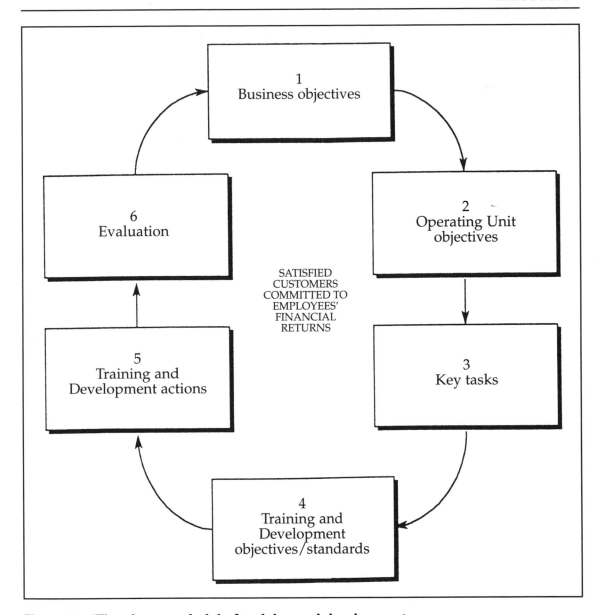

Figure 3   'The virtuous circle' of training and development

The virtuous circle is simply a way of describing the benefits to be gained from recognizing and acting on the development needs of individuals in relation to the business objectives.

Developing our earlier theme of the four Investors in People Principles as a loop around the achievement of satisfied customers, committed employees, and financial returns, the virtuous circle can be represented by Figure 3.

What do your employees think of you?

Before going any further, you might like to ask some of your employees to complete the short questionnaire shown in Figure 4, and compare their answers.

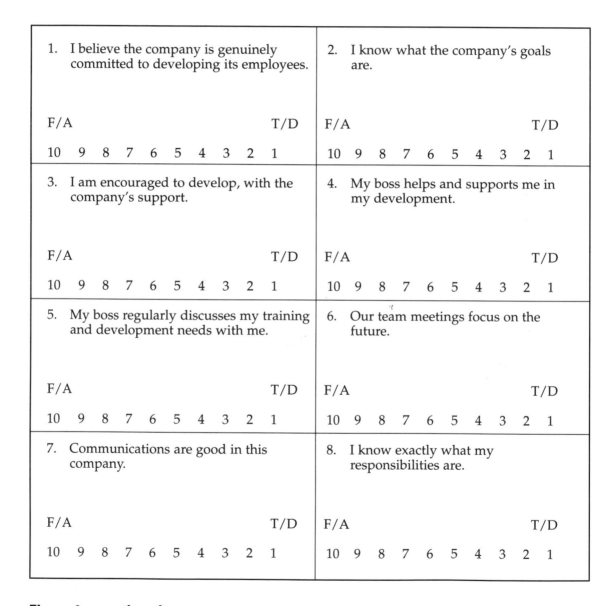

1. I believe the company is genuinely committed to developing its employees.	2. I know what the company's goals are.
F/A T/D 10 9 8 7 6 5 4 3 2 1	F/A T/D 10 9 8 7 6 5 4 3 2 1
3. I am encouraged to develop, with the company's support.	4. My boss helps and supports me in my development.
F/A T/D 10 9 8 7 6 5 4 3 2 1	F/A T/D 10 9 8 7 6 5 4 3 2 1
5. My boss regularly discusses my training and development needs with me.	6. Our team meetings focus on the future.
F/A T/D 10 9 8 7 6 5 4 3 2 1	F/A T/D 10 9 8 7 6 5 4 3 2 1
7. Communications are good in this company.	8. I know exactly what my responsibilities are.
F/A T/D 10 9 8 7 6 5 4 3 2 1	F/A T/D 10 9 8 7 6 5 4 3 2 1

Figure 4 *continued on next page*

9. I feel encouraged to put forward ideas for improving the way we do things. F/A T/D 10 9 8 7 6 5 4 3 2 1	10. Our team meetings are informative and effective. F/A T/D 10 9 8 7 6 5 4 3 2 1
11. I feel part of the team. F/A T/D 10 9 8 7 6 5 4 3 2 1	12. The company brings out the best in its people. F/A T/D 10 9 8 7 6 5 4 3 2 1
13. The company has a clear future direction. F/A T/D 10 9 8 7 6 5 4 3 2 1	14. Before *and* after I do any training, my boss helps me to understand how it will help me in my job. F/A T/D 10 9 8 7 6 5 4 3 2 1

Figure 4   The 'mini-survey': a simple tool for use in preparing for Investors in People. ('F/A' stands for 'fully agree' and 'T/D' means 'totally disagree'.) The questionnaire is intended to stimulate discussion with a group of around five people.

The questionnaire can be presented on a sheet of computer labels. You can try this with groups of around five people. Each individual completes the questionnaire anonymously, then you peel the labels off and stick them on a sheet of flip chart, marked up as a grid, as shown in Figure 5. They, and you, will probably be surprised at the variation in agreement on the 14 statements. More to the point, you can discuss the reasons for the variances and for particularly high or low scores – and ask the respondents for their ideas for improvement.

	Responses									
	10	9	8	7	6	5	4	3	2	1
1										
2										
3										
4										
5										
6										
Statements 7										
8										
9										
10										
11										
12										
13										
14										

Figure 5 **'Mini-survey' analysis grid: make up a summary grid for the sticky labels on a flipchart, with numbers 1 to 14 down the left margin to represent the 14 statements, and numbers 10 down to 1 along the top, to help you position the labels in accordance with the scores allocated by the group members. It will take about ten minutes to place the labels in their appropriate positions. Give the group something else to work on while you are doing this, such as asking them to write down three things they would do to improve how the organization develops its people. You can then run a discussion about the reasons for agreement or disagreement between the responses to the questionnaire, followed by discussion of their ideas for improvement.**

1 Business Benefits of Investors in People

We hear a good deal these days about the 'learning organization'. The ideas that underlie the learning organization are strikingly congruent with the principles of Investors in People.

The learning organization concept likens the organization to a living organism. We all know that organisms that do not adapt die sooner or later – the process of evolution and survival of the fittest. Organizations that do not adapt to change are likely to suffer the same fate. The one-time giants of the industrial and commercial world who are no longer with us are a testimony to this. Such organizations seem to have forgotten how to learn. It has been called the 'past success, future failure' syndrome. I call it corporate constipation.

The concept of the learning organization is that, to survive and grow, your organization will have to learn and adapt at a pace at least as great as change, and ideally faster. This can be summed up neatly in the formula shown in Figure 6, based on the work of Reg Revans, where L = Learning and C = Change.

$$L \geq C$$

Figure 6 **The learning organization: to survive and grow, organizations need to learn at a pace equal to or greater than change**
Source: Reg Revans

11

Learners	Non-learners
● Go at risk	● Want definitive answers
● Don't take themselves too seriously	● Are afraid to be wrong
● Ask questions	● Are closed-minded
● Are open-minded	● Rationalize
● Are prepared to be wrong	● Nit-pick
● Tolerate ambiguity	● Quote past precedents out of context

Figure 7   Learners and non-learners. Organizations that identify with the 'learners' characteristics will probably find attainment of the Investors in People national standard somewhat less daunting than Non-learners. Non-learners, however, probably have most to gain from it, if they can learn to learn.
Source: Ian Anderson/David Hall Partnership

What kind of organization are you?

Which of the characteristics set out in Figure 7 does your organization most closely associate with? Are you closer to the learning organization characteristics in the left-hand list? Are you willing to 'go at risk' – to try new things ahead of the competition? Are you open-minded with an ability to tolerate ambiguity? If so, the development of your business through Investors in People should present you with challenges rather than major difficulties.

If you line up closer to the right, your organization may have forgotten how to learn. Investors in People will probably be more difficult for you to achieve. But it is the ideal vehicle for bringing about the change in culture that you might need. It follows that your organization stands to gain even greater value from the process involved in becoming an Investor in People.

What is the link between Investors in People and the learning organization?

Of course all this talk about learners and non-learners is simply a convenient shorthand for what really goes on inside the organization.

We all know that organizations achieve nothing. It is people that produce the results – for better or for worse. That is why people must learn continually, for their own benefit and for the survival and growth of the organization.

How can Investors in People help you to become a learning organization?

An Investor in People takes systematic steps to develop its employees, in order to improve the business. If this sounds simple and logical, it is – and that's why a growing number of organizations throughout the UK are working toward the national standard.

So what's new? For many organizations, not much. These are the lots of organizations that already recognize the business benefits of developing their people, and have probably been doing it that way for years. For example, I visited a small company a few months back and spoke individually to about 25 employees, out of a total workforce of around 90. Unprompted, about eight or nine of them told me there was nothing new in Investors in People. 'This is the way Lawrence (the MD) has always worked', they said. Needless to say, this is a highly successful company – and now a recognized Investor in People.

What Investors in People offers organizations like this is an opportunity to take stock of the way they develop their human resources and to put in place mechanisms for continual improvement. It also offers the opportunity for public recognition of their good practice, if they want that. For others – those that have not yet 'seen the light' – Investors in People offers them a very practical way of starting down the road of improving business performance through developing their people.

Realizing that Investors in People is not about training for the sake of it is crucial. It is about looking at where your business is heading and taking action to get there, by investing in your most valuable asset – your people. It really makes no sense to keep employees in the dark and subject them to 'mushroom management' (see cartoon following).

How will it improve your business?

Organizations become successful by:

● Developing new markets, or
● Improving on what they already do.

Either way, significant, sustainable gains can only be made through people. Even technology has its limits. It doesn't matter how fast the microprocessor becomes if your operations are constrained by systems or people.

'The dark and ancient art of mushroom management.'

● People are the only means of sustained business development;
● People are the only means of making your systems work better.

You have probably been frustrated at one time or another by the apparent inability of your systems – take for example, your information technology system – to produce what you think it might be capable of. Investing in a more powerful, more sophisticated package will be a waste of money without investing in the skills and abilities of your people to use it more effectively.

Blindingly obvious, isn't it? But how good is your organization at making that kind of investment in skills, so as to add *real* value to your operations? The investment in training and development in a situation

14

like this would be laughably low compared to the value it could add. Perhaps that is the real reason why managers in some organizations do not give much thought to training – because they feel that, compared to the key capital programmes they are responsible for, the sums of money involved are hardly worth bothering about.

Perhaps the leverage potential has never occurred to them. If I offered you a return of, say, 2 to 1 on your investment – double your money – would you be interested? OK. So let's make sure *they* are!

The 1994 evaluation of the first three years of Investors in People in England and Wales reported that most of the organizations involved had made significant changes to their work practices. This has already led to improved business performance in a number of cases. Benefits cited include increased employee motivation and better targeting of training and development activities.

Much wider benefits can also accrue to organizations, the following examples giving some idea of what is possible:

- An oil company in north east Scotland publicized the fact that it had achieved Investors in People recognition and immediately saw a dramatic improvement in the quality of people applying for jobs there;
- A bakery and retail business has witnessed average spend per customer rise consistently over recent years, due to the increased quality of its products and customer service – all achieved through training;
- Recognized as an Investor in People, a small engineering company found itself talked about in the same breath as some of the biggest names in the industrial world, making it significantly more attractive to potential customers;
- A small computer systems supplier in the West of Scotland reported a 27 per cent increase in sales immediately after an in-house development programme involving all staff.

Isn't it just another government scheme?

No, far from it.

Investors in People offers the most potent business development opportunity. There are many approaches to developing business; there are probably more books per metre of shelf space on this subject than on any other aspect of management. The thread running through all of these approaches is people. So, shouldn't you be cutting through the theory and getting down to the real people issues? If you do that, your people will probably solve half your problems for you.

Investors in People is not a scheme or a programme. It is a flexible framework that helps you develop your business, by building on key strengths. But you have to adapt it to meet the needs of your business if you want to get the maximum value from it.

What does it involve?

Put simply, Investors in People requires you to assess where your organization is heading, what contribution individuals need to make to achieve your business goals, and how they can be developed to make their contributions more effective.

If you are already doing that effectively, then you are probably running a successful organization. Investors offers a framework to help you continue to improve. If you are not doing it, it is time you started – for the sake of your business, and the people you employ.

How much work will it involve?

Investors in People is simply a framework that will help you assess whether your people and your management systems are adding value to the business. It will help you to recognize how these can be improved, and decide what additional action you need to take. Anything you do will be entirely appropriate to your business needs. You decide. It will create a mass of bureaucracy only if you allow it to.

The checklist on page xvii may already have given you some food for thought on how well you develop your people to develop your business. Now consider the following:

- Do you know where you want your organization to be three to five years from now, or are you making it up as you go along?
- Are your senior colleagues truly clear on this? How do you know? If they are not completely clear, how can you expect the rest of your workforce to be?
- Have your objectives been translated into a written plan? Is the plan used to drive the business? How often do you review the plan in the light of market forces?
- Have you let your employees at all levels know exactly what your objectives are? Are you sure you have done this effectively? How do you know?
- Do you regularly review the skills your employees – including your managers – need to meet your objectives? Or do you prefer to fly the organization by the seat of your pants?
- Do you set aside resources to meet the training and development needs of your employees, in line with your business plan? Have

you any idea what you are spending on training and development? It may be more than you think, so shouldn't you be making sure you are getting value for money?

- Have you introduced induction programmes for your new recruits? Or do they just muddle through? How might this have affected employee turnover?
- Have most of your employees been given some form of training/development – in line with your business objectives – within the last 12 months? If not, was this a management decision, or simply default?
- Do you assess the results of training and development activities? Do you ask questions to help establish whether the action you took was the best way of developing the individual? Do you assess whether the training or development has helped the individual to do the job better? How has this helped your business in practical terms?
- Do you keep simple records of who has been trained/developed and in what areas? Or do you have a brain like a supercomputer?
- Do you ask your people what they think about the way the organization is run? And do you really care about what they tell you?
- Do you ask your people for their ideas to improve the business? Do you act on them? Do you realize what a powerful business development tool this can be?

Nobody starts from zero. You should be able to respond positively to some of these questions. If you can not, how on earth have you managed to stay in business?

Now use the practical sections, temperature checks and examples in the book to develop simple systems to plug the gaps. You are already on the way to becoming an Investor in People. And, more important, to improving your business.

2 But we already have ISO9000!

The challenges facing your organization over the next few years will require the maximum input from your people, combined with a drive to maintain and build on the levels of quality and customer care that you have established so far. You might already have a recognized quality standard such as ISO9000, or some other industry-based award. I will look at the ISO9000 standard throughout this chapter, but the principles apply to other quality standards also and it is therefore useful to make some comparisons with Investors in People.

If you already have ISO9000 – or if you are working towards it – you might find it helpful to reflect on the similarities and differences between it and Investors in People. Think about it. How can you possibly maintain these quality standards if you do not continuously develop your people?

How Investors in People compares and integrates with ISO9000

ISO9000 was introduced as a solution to the poor level of quality and the volume of rejection/rework prevalent in many parts of the manufacturing sector. The concept is well recognized. Build quality in at every stage of the process, from the raw materials, right through to the delivered product and support services provided to the end user, by having people take ownership of the process at every stage. The result? Improved margins through drastically reduced rework, returns and customer complaints. Well, that's the theory. ...

ISO9000 has become increasingly accepted in manufacturing, and also in non-manufacturing sectors. The pioneers of ISO9000 in the service industries found the translation of practices and terminology to their businesses difficult, but many have made the standard fit their operations. More recent adopters of the standard in the service sectors have an abundance of case history from which to learn.

Organizations that have attained ISO9000 registration have experienced mixed results. Some have found themselves burdened with additional bureaucracy and cost, with no significant improvement in quality (what has been called the 'concrete life-jacket' syndrome). Others have used it to add measurable value to the business, by tightening up systems and sharpening their people's focus on quality.

Using ISO9000 to advantage

The main benefits cited by companies that have used ISO9000 to advantage include:

- Standardization of work practices within the organization;
- Greater efficiency in manufacturing and service activities;
- Reduced levels of rejects, rework and returned goods;
- Greater customer satisfaction;
- Improved control of the business;
- Enhanced competitiveness;
- Improved profitability.

What's in it for you?

The key question is 'Will achieving ISO9000 deliver more business and make us more profitable?' The answer to this depends on the answers to two further sets of questions:

Operating efficiency

- Will the processes involved in working towards the standard make your organization more efficient?
- Will the introduction of quality systems ensure that each employee knows what they are expected to do and to what standard, so that there is a consistent approach across the organization?
- Will it assist flexibility of operation, where new employees can reach maximum efficiency more quickly through following standard practices?

If you cannot answer these three questions positively and commit yourself to making it work for you, then you must seriously challenge the need to achieve the ISO9000 standard. But remember, some organizations do use it to good effect.

Business development

- Will achievement of ISO9000 make the organization more attractive to customers and potential customers?
- Will your customers begin to demand ISO9000 registration as a prerequisite of bidding for contracts?
- Are your competitors doing it?

The Investors in People national standard

Investors in People has been agreed by the Confederation of British Industry (CBI), the Trades Union Congress (TUC), and other leading organizations in the field of business development and human resource development. It is founded on:

- Sharing the business mission and objectives with all members of the workforce;
- Being clear on what each individual is expected to do to achieve these objectives;
- Developing the workforce in order to achieve business objectives;
- Evaluating the effectiveness of these processes, and the impact on the business.

Although Investors in People starts from a different philosophy, the benefits cited from companies that have achieved the Investors in People national standard – and some that are currently working towards it – are similar to those experienced by companies that have successfully introduced ISO9000.

In fact, the two standards are entirely compatible, and many companies embrace both. The point is that, whatever standards you adopt, they must be taking you in the same direction.

Either, both, or none?

The question remains as to whether you should commit to achieving ISO9000, Investors in People, or both. Or indeed whether to remain on the outside. It is not a simple question to answer, because:

21

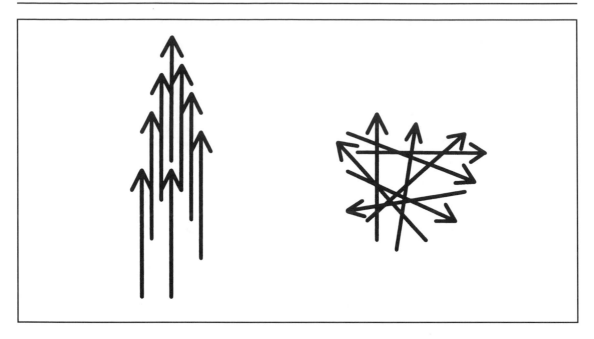

Figure 8   Are your systems for developing people and developing quality pointing in the same direction? Or are your people totally bemused by it all?

- Both philosophies and approaches apply, to one degree or another, to your organization;
- Both are rigorous. ISO9000 has the reputation – perhaps unfairly – of being bureaucratic. It is true to say that it is systems driven, but also true that many companies have found the process of developing these systems beneficial to the business. Although Investors in People need not be heavily paper-based, particularly in small to medium companies, systems do have to be in place, and seen to be working effectively;
- Both approaches are based on the concept of continuous improvement. Although the re-assessment requirements of Investors in People might seem less onerous than those for ISO9000 they both require, in effect, that a continuous process of review exists as an integral part of managing the business.

ISO9000 is becoming mandatory for companies wishing to do business in many sectors. That situation may affect you right now, or may be some years away.

Investors in People is some way behind in that sense, but there are early signs that larger companies might make recognition as an Investor in People a condition of doing business with them. It is impossible to forecast. What is clear is the definite growth of interest in Investors in

People, driven by the ambitious government targets for education and training, referred to earlier.

One final thought on Investors in People and ISO9000. I know several organizations that have achieved ISO9000 and then gone on to become Investors in People. With hindsight, they have told me that they wish they had done it the other way round, because working towards Investors in People would have been more effective in getting people to understand what quality management is all about.

3 Why and How People Learn

If you are to get real business benefits from Investors in People, consider the context in which people learn and develop. To understand people's motivations for learning, we need to know something of the human condition in relation to work.

Why do *you* go to work? If it's your own company, why are you running it?

Of course, the first answer is usually money. But is that always the prime motivator? Emphatically not, judging from the hundreds of people I have asked over the years. Ask half a dozen people this same question and you can expect at least half a dozen different answers. Have you ever asked your people why they work for you? Perhaps you think you know. Maybe you don't want to hear.

When I ask this question, people are usually glib in their answers at first. They will almost always say 'money', but, when asked to put money aside, they suggest such motivations as:

- Being treated fairly;
- Doing the job right;
- Credit for doing a good job;
- Security;
- Recognition – as an individual, not a clock number;
- Working in a good team;
- Advancement – to a more challenging role (not necessarily promotion);
- Working for a boss that they respect.

This is basic. You will find it covered in any course for first line supervisors. The simple logic and wisdom of this is seldom disputed. You don't dispute it, do you? So why do so many organizations and managers fail to act on it? If you have not asked your people why they work for you, you cannot know what really makes them tick. If you do not know what makes them tick, how can you help them to help you develop your business?

- Is it safe to assume that the order in which *you* would place the above factors would be the same as your employees?
- Would *all* of your people place them in the same order?
- Do individuals' motivations remain the same throughout their lives?

The answer to all three questions is 'Of course not!'

Don't assume that your view of life and work is shared by others. People are individuals and it is a big mistake to treat them as one homogenous mass. Consider how your own attitude to various aspects of your life and work have changed as you:

- Age
- Marry
- Have children
- Divorce
- Become richer or poor
- Experience personal happiness or tragedy
- And so on.

Figure 9 portrays a few of the influences that affect individual attitudes to work, and the effect of time and experience on the individual's order of priorities. Consider how your own priorities have changed as life 'rolls along'. What comes at the top of the wheel now? Is it the same as last year? How might events and experience change your priorities in the coming years?

If you need convincing, here's a simple way of proving people's individuality. Look at Figure 10. How many squares are there? Once you have studied it and made up your mind how many squares there are, show it to any group of people and then compare their answers. Are they all the same? I bet they are not. And this is just a simple diagram. Now, can you really assume that everyone sees work and life in the same way? Every single member of your workforce is unique. How many squares? Forget it, it's not important. It's differences in the individual perception that matters.

Here's a story that illustrates the great chasm that often exists, quite needlessly, between management and the workforce. I recently took part in the strategic review of a medium sized company. As you might expect, the job involved interviewing people in various parts of the organization. I had a group discussion with five or six great big guys ('bears' as we would call them in Glasgow). They had come straight off site, and sat there in muddy overalls while I introduced myself and told them why I wanted to talk to them. When I finished, and handed over to them, one of them said 'Right, I want to get this off my chest straight away. Why did we not get an invite to the Christmas dance last year?' I held back, expecting his mates to ridicule him, but they supported him to a man.

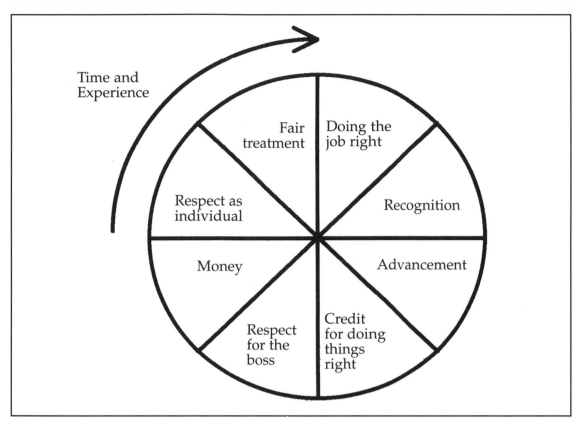

Figure 9 **Some factors that affect individual motivation. What comes at the top? How do time and individual experience change priorities?**

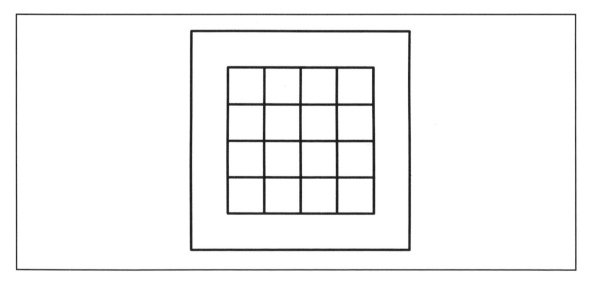

Figure 10 **How many squares?**

Over the next hour or so, we covered many things that they felt were 'wrong with the company' including money matters, of course. Some of these were (in my view) more valid than others. When I later carried out some further investigation, I found that the Christmas dance issue was not quite as straightforward as it first appeared, but that is another story. The point is this. Why would half a dozen adults put that at the top of their list of things to raise with me? More to the point, why hadn't management realized how excluded they felt? Simply because they saw them as 'the bears'? They wouldn't be interested in a Christmas party – would they?

Individuals as learners

Peoples' approaches to the learning process are as individual as they are themselves. That is another reason why you need to talk to your people, to find out:

● What they need to learn, and
● The best way for them to do it.

Successful organizations show respect for people by finding creative solutions to their development needs. The good news is that these approaches are often much more cost effective than just packing people off to training courses.

So don't make the mistake of assuming that everyone will learn in the same way. Some people devour books. Give them some written material and they will learn away. Others are much happier being taken through it step by step, and there are probably 101 other ways. You need to think about how to make the learning experience as effective as possible. This is yet another reason for evaluating your training and development actions, so you can see which approaches work best.

Some of the many options for developing people, in a cost-effective and time-effective way, are discussed in Chapter 8. Remember, it's your business and your people we are talking about. You need to find the solutions that are best for you.

4 Commitment

In this chapter and the three that follow, we look at the four Principles and the 24 Indicators in detail. We consider what the Indicators mean, some of the options available to meet them, and how some organizations have tackled them.

> ## An Investor in People makes a public commitment from the top to develop all employees to achieve its business objectives.
>
> ● Every employer should have a written but flexible plan which sets out business goals and targets, considers how employees will contribute to achieving the plan and specifies how development needs in particular will be assessed and met.
>
> ● Management should develop and communicate to all employees a vision of where the organization is going and the contribution employees will make to its success, involving employee representatives as appropriate.

Indicator 1.1 *There is a public commitment from the most senior level within the organization to develop people*

In 1993 I visited a small engineering company in central Scotland. There was an Investors in People statement of intent hanging on the wall, in the reception area. It had been signed by the managing director. I noticed that it was almost hidden by a potted plant. When I asked the MD who had moved the plant in front of the certificate, he coughed in

'Do I look like the kind of person who wouldn't be committed to developing people?'

embarrassment. 'Now you mention it', he said, 'that plant was only four feet tall when we put the certificate up on the wall.'

How much had they progressed towards becoming Investors in People? Not a lot, as you might expect. If I had stopped employees as they walked through the reception area and asked them to give me the gist of what was on that certificate, do you think they could have told me?

If I came into your organization today and asked some of your people if they believe top management is committed to their development, what would they tell me?

I know one manufacturing company where the four Principles are displayed on enormous notices throughout the plant. Rather naively, I asked some of the employees if they believed in management's commitment to their training and development. They almost ran me out of town.

The commitment has to be *alive and kicking*.

How to do it

'Public' means letting your people know – although you can make it public to the world if you want to! Here are a few possibilities. None of them, as you will see, is particularly exotic, so there can be little excuse for not doing them – for the good of your business.

● Communicate!;
● Tell your people about your commitment to them;
● Tell them how important their development is to the business, and to their own future;
● Put notices up on the walls;
● Give people copies of memos stating your commitment – signed by the MD or chair;
● Put it in your employee newsletter;
● Make sure it is on the agenda for team meetings;
● Review it regularly at board meetings – do people know about your commitment? Do they believe it? How do you know?;
● Tell them again – and again.

This all sounds wonderfully glib, doesn't it? I offer no apology. You will achieve very little with a grand gesture from the top of the house and nothing to follow it. One of the most frequent comments I hear from employees is that management starts things off with a great fanfare, and then fails to follow them through. The initiative, whatever it might be, is then seen as 'flavour of the month'.

That will not sign up your employees for Investors in People – or, more important, help you develop the business. If you do not communicate with your people – especially in times of uncertainty and change – they will make up their own stories, possibly to the detriment of your business. Communicate your commitment to your people as often as you can.

In one organization I know, each of the six directors has been assigned the task of talking to a random sample of three or four people every month, to get feedback on the effectiveness of the company's communications. The results are discussed at board meetings. Is this a good approach? I think so – well it's a good start at least. Could you do it? Could you improve on it? I'm sure you could.

An important point to remember – there are really two types of commitment:

● The first is the public commitment you make to the development of your people, not to Investors in People itself. You can of course mention Investors in People, or you may prefer to play it down in the early stages, if you feel your employees will be discouraged by what might appear to be yet another initiative.

● The second is the formal Investors in People commitment you make to your LEC or TEC. This is usually in the form of a letter from your chief executive to the chief executive of the LEC or TEC. Often, the LEC/TEC will issue a certificate of commitment, which you can display on the wall if you want to. Most organizations display the certificate, when they feel the time is right.

Remember that in terms of 'public commitment', it is the former – the commitment to developing your people – that is important.

Temperature check ✓

	YES	NO
If an assessor came into my organization today my chief executive would give a credible account of our training and development practices.	☐	☐
If the assessor asked employees what they thought of top management's commitment to their development, their responses would be positive.	☐	☐
This organization's commitment to developing its people is alive and kicking.	☐	☐

WHAT ACTION DO YOU NEED TO TAKE?

Indicator 1.2 *Employees at all levels are aware of the broad aims or vision of the organization*

I am sometimes pleasantly surprised by the level of understanding among employees, of the organization's future direction, although not as often as I would like.

I visited a small family-owned group of hotels, employing about 100 people, about a year ago. When I consulted employees individually, they were all able to tell me roughly what the mission statement said. So far, so good. I asked them if they believed it, or if it was just words on paper. Virtually all of them could tell me what it meant for them, and where they fitted into the company's vision. Clearly, management had invested in making sure their people know what the business is about.

How to do it

Develop a mission statement

In all but the tiniest organizations, I recommend a mission or vision statement. You don't have to have one to satisfy this Indicator, but what better way to express your future direction? Don't let the terminology put you off. Mission and vision statements are essentially the same thing, stated in slightly different terms. You can call it anything you want – what about 'our aim/our goals' or similar?

Let's deal with the biggest problem straight away. Many people – including senior managers – are highly sceptical about mission statements. This is usually because the statement does not ring true. I have seen some that almost made me want to throw up, particularly in the last few years as more and more organizations have jumped on the mission statement bandwagon, without giving it sufficient thought. How can you expect people to give their best for you if even the senior managers are not convinced?

Ask yourself:

● Would the mission or vision statement I have just prepared make my people fall about laughing?
● Why? Is it because they need convincing about the mission itself? Or is it just a lousy mission statement?

Try to make it fit the way you do business, and avoid the meaningless jargon and highly suspect value statements that some organizations seem drawn to. You can do something about convincing your employees to sign up for an understandable and believable mission, but you are in for a hard time if they think it is just another load of management codswallop.

Wouldn't the process of drawing up a mission or vision statement help you to think more clearly about the future direction of the business? Wouldn't it be a good way of letting your employees – and your customers – know that you are serious about the business, and about them?

I also suggest that:

- Your mission statement should make clear reference to developing your people;
- You should include a brief statement of your main goals – for employees, but not for public display. You can be quite selective in the information you include here. You do not have to include sensitive information such as financial targets, although some organizations are quite open about these;
- Employees should be given personal copies;
- You should post it on the walls or notice boards;
- You should check frequently that it is current. I frequently go into organizations and find they have a couple of versions of the mission statement floating around. The result is obvious – people don't know which one is current, and dismiss the whole thing as a paper exercise;
- Ensure it is properly displayed. Replace dog-eared copies. It's your employees you are addressing, and they are important;
- You should continually reinforce the mission/vision/goals in communicating with employees.

Reinforcing the Mission

Here is an excellent illustration of how the mission or vision can be used to drive training and development actions. The group of hotels I mentioned earlier has a smart cordon bleu restaurant, where customers pay premium prices for high quality food and service.

I was curious to know how the restaurant manager managed to instil a feeling for quality in his employees, particularly those who had gained earlier experience with other companies.

Using the example of setting a table for dinner, he told me that he would ask a new trainee to set up the table according to his instructions, and then review the results with the trainee, along the lines of 'Now John, I want you to look at what you've done, and tell me how you think it squares with our mission of providing the highest possible quality of dining experience for our guests. Do you think that perhaps the cutlery set slightly out of line, and the napkin ring not quite in the middle of the napkin are in keeping with our mission? Would you like to try again please?'

Incidentally, he reinforces this with a colour photograph of what a properly set table in his restaurant should look like.

'CHARGE!'

The real test is whether your people are *aware* of your broad aims or vision. You do not need to have a mission statement to achieve that, but you will have to communicate clearly, effectively and frequently. Otherwise, when you charge at the competition, you might find your people some way behind.

An example of a mission statement is given by Figure 11. It is for that well known company, the XYZ Optical Manufacturing Co Ltd, so it is unlikely you will want to copy it. You will have to write your own.

I have tried to avoid the usual hollow statements such as 'simply the best', and so on. In addition a statement of goals would probably be attached – for example: volume turnover, increased market share, new product developments, and so on. But whatever you do, remember the KISS principle – keep it short and simple.

The XYZ Optical Manufacturing Co Ltd

Our Mission

The XYZ Optical Manufacturing Company aims to be one of the three foremost European suppliers of optical equipment to the scientific research sector in Europe, within the next two years.

We will achieve that position by:

providing the highest quality of products and service to our customers;

researching new technologies, processes and materials; and

continuously investing in the skills and abilities of our workforce.

Figure 11   Sample mission statement

Involving your employees in developing the mission statement

Why not involve your employees – perhaps a small group of them – in devising the mission statement? You will be surprised at what they contribute. You will probably find their ideas helpful, and employees are more likely to support it if they know some of their colleagues had a hand in preparing it.

Alternatively, ask all employees for their suggestions on what should go into the mission statement. This is commendable, but you will probably get so many different versions that you will have a difficult job sorting it out. If you do want to go down this road, it would probably be better to ask each employee to write down one or two key words that should go into the mission statement, and construct it around those most commonly quoted.

Temperature check ✓

	YES	NO
A visitor coming into our organization today would be struck by the knowledge and understanding our people have of our mission.	☐	☐
Employees would be able to tell visitors what our main goals are.	☐	☐
Employees really believe in our mission/vision.	☐	☐
We have involved our people in devising the mission statement.	☐	☐
We use our mission as a focus for all our training and development activities.	☐	☐
Although we don't have a mission statement, our employees are all clear on our mission/goals.	☐	☐

WHAT ACTION DO YOU NEED TO TAKE?

Indicator 1.3 *There is a written but flexible plan which sets out business goals and targets*

A large manufacturing company I visited a couple of years ago employs about 600 people and is part of a chain of manufacturing plants across Europe and the US. The MD proudly waved his business plan at me. 'So what', I thought 'why so proud of a business plan?' It turned out it was their first written business plan in over fifty years of trading. But they had managed up to now, so why bother?

According to the MD, it was stimulated by Investors in People. Had they prepared it specially for Investors? No, he told me, Investors in People had brought them to realize that they had never really planned the future direction of the company. In the current trading climate, that might make the difference between success and failure.

Over 60 per cent of companies in the UK do not have written business plans. Of those that do, I wonder how many of their plans are written for the benefit of the bank or some funder, and then consigned to the depths of the safe. Successful organizations know that a written business plan is the first step in articulating the organization's future, so that they can rally their employees to support it.

How to do it

It is the 'front end' of the written plan that concerns us for Investors in People. Here are some of the areas usually covered:

- The mission or vision of the organization (this could of course double as your mission/vision statement);
- Key products/services and markets;
- Detailed goals and targets – at various levels of the organization;
- The organization's core skills;
- The organization structure;
- Key resources – people, plant, processes, finance, and so on;
- Training and development matters, that is:
  - a statement of your policy on training and development
  - the amount of the training and development budget, as a separate heading (not hidden within the office administration budget or some other obscure heading)
  - the other resources you have allocated for training and development.

The written plan and Investors in People

For Investors in People:

- You must have a written plan or equivalent document (or documents). Help in preparing business plans is usually available from LECs and TECs. Contact your LEC or TEC for advice.
- It must be flexible. That means it must be reviewed on a regular basis, and sensitive to changes in the market place. One way of demonstrating the plan's flexibility is to include within it a statement saying how often it will be reviewed, and under what other circumstances – for example unforeseen changes in the market place, new technologies, and new legislation. This will show that the plan is a live document, and not just something prepared to satisfy the bank or some other external body.
- Indicator 1.4 requires the plan to set out the broad development needs of the workforce and specify how they will be assessed and met.

This acts as the foundation for the training and development activities that will follow.
● The resources allocated to training and development must be set out in the plan (see Indicator 2.1).

Monitoring the environment

Remember the concept of the learning organization referred to in Chapter 1? How can you become a learning organization, how can you adapt to change, how will you know what investment you need to make in your people, if you don't know what's coming at you, over the hill?

You need a system for environmental monitoring. The 'SPLICET' framework in Figure 12 covers most of the *external* changes and influences that are likely to affect any organization. (As Figure 12 shows, SPLICET stands for 'social, political, legal, institutional, competitive, economic and technological'.)

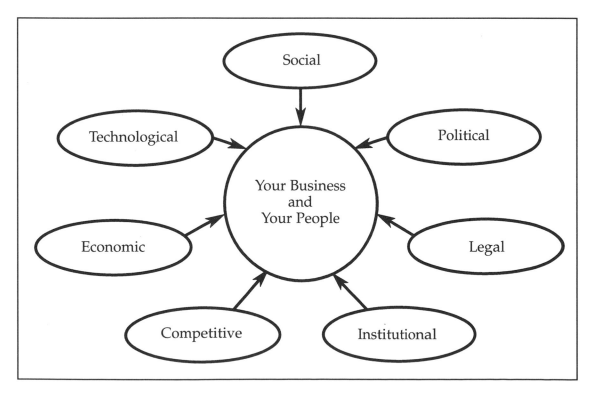

Figure 12   The 'SPLICET' framework for environmental monitoring. What training and development needs do these influences throw up?

On the face of it, you do not have to have such a system for Investors in People. But remember that Indicator 2.2 says that training and development needs must be reviewed against the business objectives. The business objectives need to be reviewed in the light of what is going on 'out there'. Otherwise, what's the point?

External influences and training/development needs

Below are a few examples of how the SPLICET framework might apply to your business. What training and development needs might these throw up? And how can you develop your people simply by involving them in environmental monitoring?

Social

Are social trends – such as changing attitudes to smoking, drinking, eating, crime, family or leisure – likely to alter your customers' attitudes to what they buy from you? What happens when your customers begin to 'surf the Internet' or take a ride down the information superhighway? How will these factors affect your business? Will they improve or worsen your employees' ability to make profitable transactions with customers? What training, information, or support will your people need to deal with this?

Political

What effect are national or local political influences likely to have on your business? Would a shift in the local or national political balance make your products/services more or less attractive? Do your people need to be politically attuned (regardless of their/your political allegiances)? What training/development do they need to help guide your business through the political rapids? What could your people do to exploit such changes?

Legal

What new legislation is passing through Parliament? Will it affect your technologies, your processes, your service delivery, your customer liability? Are your people up to date with it? Will adopting the new legislation be traumatic, or will the transition be seamless? Have you briefed your people on this? Have your competitors already got an edge over you in this area?

Institutional

> Will changes in the local infrastructure affect your business? How dependent are you on public bodies for business, for operating licences, inspections, 'bills of health', or business support activities? What would your people do if there was a sudden change in the infrastructure? Have you briefed them on what's coming?

Competitive

> Who are your competitors, where are they? Are they encroaching upon your share of the market? Do your employees realize the importance of this sort of market intelligence? Do they act as 'lookouts' to help you make sure the competition is not sneaking up on you? Have you briefed them? Do you get regular feedback? Are your competitors better at this than you?

Economic

> What economic pressures are likely to affect your customers' buying patterns? Are you able to cut costs without cutting quality? Do you know you can rely on your people when the going gets tough? Have you engaged their brains on finding ways to improve efficiency?

Technological

> Are you about to spend serious money on some shiny new kit, but nothing on training your people to use it? Are there technology enhancements out there that you could benefit from at minimal cost (for example software applications)? Are your people curious to seek out and explore them? Have you briefed/trained them to do this? Have you sent them out to look?

Involving your people in environmental monitoring

How often do you stop to 'sniff the air'? How can you find the time to do it when you have your head down, running the organization? Could you use some help – some extra 'lookouts'?

Successful organizations involve their people in environmental monitoring of some kind. It might just be a matter of looking out for competitors' vans when they are out on the road to get some idea of where the competition is working, plugging into their 'pub network', or undertaking fact-finding assignments in new technologies or production methods. I am not talking just about managers. Many organizations involve employees at various levels in environmental monitoring.

The point of all this is to help you steer the business, and keep abreast of the training and development implications. Involvement in such activities is also a worthwhile development process for employees in its own right.

Temperature check ✓

	YES	NO
Our people are clear on the organization's future direction.	☐	☐
We are tightly focused on bringing our products/services to the market.	☐	☐
We have set goals and targets for all relevant parts of the business.	☐	☐
Our business plan is a working document, which helps us to focus our resources on achieving our mission.	☐	☐
We have developed our employees as lookouts for the business.	☐	☐

WHAT ACTION DO YOU NEED TO TAKE?

Indicator 1.4 *The plan identifies broad development needs and specifies how they will be assessed and met*

This links closely with Indicator 1.3, and what follows should be read in conjunction with the guidance given there. It is a vital part of the Investors in People process. It amounts to saying:

- We know where we want to be (our vision/mission/goals) . . .
- We know what resources we have at our disposal . . .
- We recognize our core skills and competences . . .
- Here are the broad areas in which we need to develop our people . . .

- Here's how we will assess these needs in greater detail ...
- And here's how we will meet them.

What is called for is a broad statement of development needs and your approach to assessing and meeting them. This will lay the foundation for the more detailed analysis you will carry out under Principle 2 and the actions you will take within Principle 3. A hypothetical example of how I would approach it is given below.

How to do it

Imagine I am running a small business consultancy company based in Scotland. I want to gain a bigger share of the Scottish market, and have

---

Our 1996/7 business plan requires us to:

- Achieve a 5 per cent increase in our share of the UK business consultancy market at existing margins;
- Explore opportunities in the in-company executive training market in the US (New York City) with a recovery of market entry costs within 6 months.

This will require efficiency gains to enable us to secure and fulfil orders from these markets profitably. We must:

- Make our sales presentations more effective;
- Improve our use of information technology for this purpose;
- Develop the negotiating and selling skills of the team;
- Develop a detailed understanding of market conditions in New York.

We will concentrate our training and development efforts during the life of this business plan in the above areas, through:

- External sales training courses;
- Off-the-job instruction in the use of graphics software from an experienced member of the team;
- A personal development project carried out by two team members to gauge the market in New York.

Before taking these actions, we will review specific needs, targets and standards by discussion with individual employees, at least twice a year.

Figure 13   Linking broad development needs to the business plan – an example

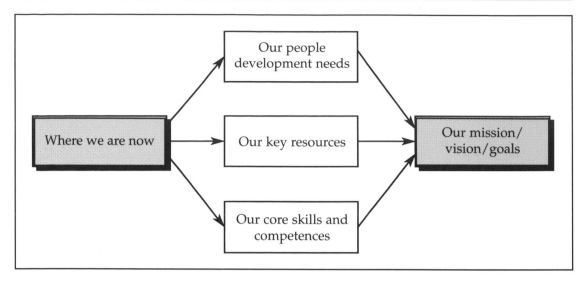

Figure 14   Moving from current reality to the vision, by considering the development needs of people

seen an opportunity to develop new work in the USA. This part of my business plan would look something like the example shown in Figure 13. Don't let the numbers distract you from the key issue of linking broad development needs with the business objectives, which is what Investors in People requires.

Figure 14, which owes much to Lou Tice, puts the identification of broad training and development needs in context with the business mission/vision, key resources and core skills. Detailed analysis of training and development needs at the individual level is discussed under Indicator 2.3. (Also see Temperature check opposite.)

Indicator 1.5 *The employer has considered what employees at all levels will contribute to the success of the organization and has communicated this effectively to them*

This is another area where I am sometimes pleasantly surprised. When I ask people if they understand their roles and responsibilities, and how they fit with other members of the team, I often find they are clearer on these than I expected. This is not altogether surprising – it would be a

---

> ## Temperature check ✓
>
> | | YES | NO |
> |---|---|---|
> | If an assessor called today, we would be able to explain clearly the link between our business plan and our training/development activities. | ☐ | ☐ |
> | This linkage is set out clearly in the business plan itself. | ☐ | ☐ |
> | The areas for training set out in the business plan will help us to achieve our objectives. | ☐ | ☐ |
> | The written plan and the training and development needs flowing from it are reviewed roughly every three months. | ☐ | ☐ |
>
> ### WHAT ACTION DO YOU NEED TO TAKE?

very odd organization where the van driver, the secretary and the pickle slicer didn't know who is supposed to do what. I don't imagine your organization is like that. Is it?

How to do it

There are various ways of ensuring that people are clear on the individual contributions they are expected to make to the success of the organization. The possibilities can be presented under two main headings – verbal and written:

- *Verbal instruction and communication* – allocating tasks, reminders, coaching and support from managers, supervisors or experienced workers, regular team or individual meetings, and so on.
- *Written systems* – job descriptions, key task lists, standard operating procedures, operating manuals, and so on.

Verbal instruction and communication

Many organizations, particularly small companies with simple structures, manage perfectly well without producing reams of written instructions. I know one organization where the manager sits down each week for a brief discussion with each individual, to review last week's performance, plan the week ahead, and anticipate any problems likely to arise. And in another organization, the manager has a short coffee meeting with everyone first thing every morning. This is highly informal, and people are as likely to chat about last night's episode of 'Coronation Street' as how the new software package is coming along. The point is, in each case – it works.

Don't tell me you don't have the time to do it. These organizations are no different from yours. They are subject to the same pressures as you, but see continuous communication as a worthwhile investment – because it involves everyone in driving the business, and saves time in the long run.

Written systems

Verbal approaches often need to be underpinned by written systems, because the nature of the operation or the size and complexity of the organization requires it. Clearly, even in very small organizations, the difference between, for example, manufacturing and retailing, or the fact that employees are located at three sites rather than one, might make a difference to the approach you adopt.

But, again, the process does not have to be unduly complicated. For instance in one small hotel I'm familiar with new staff are introduced to the list of key tasks and checks that must be carried out at the beginning of each shift. The main person responsible is shown against each task, and there are clear procedures to ensure cover if that person is off duty. Dead simple, but it works.

You may of course have standard operating procedures, perhaps as part of a recognized quality system.

What are the ten most important things your employees need to know? Are you repeatedly frustrated at the constant interruptions, or phone calls to you at home on your day off, to ask you about these? Why not write them down in very simple terms, and make sure everyone knows how to find the information they need? That might save you being interrupted, and the business grinding to a halt when you are supposed to be practising your swing. It will, more to the point, help your people look good in front of customers, because they will have the knowledge they need at their finger-tips. This, in turn, will make them feel better about themselves and about their contribution to the business, which will further feed their motivation to do better.

Of course, in many cases the information needs of your people will be more complex than that. The point I am making is simply that you can build up straightforward, effective systems for very little effort, which will save you time and heartache in the longer term. Why not ask your experienced people to write them for you? Wouldn't that also be good development for them?

Job descriptions

I would particularly like to examine the use of job descriptions as one way of setting out individual contributions to the business. I realize that they are not everybody's idea of a good time, but many organizations have used them successfully for years. Some say they do more harm than good, because people will work exclusively within them, and will not go beyond them to benefit the business. Frankly, that is a cop out. If that happens, you badly need to look at other complementary approaches to make sure that everyone is contributing effectively to the business.

If, for example, you run a small retail branch and frequently find employees standing doing very little during quiet periods, when you know that the display stands need to be smartened up, surely you should make it clear that the standard of branch presentation is everyone's responsibility? You could of course write that in to everyone's job description. But the point is, by making it clear that everyone has a role to play in certain areas of the business, you need not suffer people sticking rigidly to their job descriptions. It is your business after all, and you're paying them!

A well written job description will help nonetheless to encourage employees to go the extra mile. You do not have to have job descriptions for Investors in People. But what better way to set out clearly what the individual is supposed to do to help achieve the business objectives? Except for the tiniest organizations every individual should have a job description, or at least there should be generic descriptions covering each type of job.

The traditional components of a job description are:

- Job title
- Main purpose of the job
- Who the individual reports to
- Main tasks or areas of responsibility.

Some job descriptions – usually for managers – give limits of authority, for example, to commit the company to expenditure up to a given level, or to deal with customer complaints without referring to a higher authority. For a more focused job description, I would add:

- A summary of the organization's objectives, from the written plan
- Individual objectives flowing from the business objectives
- The basic competences needed to achieve these objectives

- Performance criteria (for example, the level of sales or production against which performance will be measured).

Don't miss the opportunity to write managers' responsibilities for training and development into their job descriptions – the need for this will become clearer as we look at other Indicators.

Believe it or not, all of the above can be covered on one side of A4 paper. I have seen some excellent examples which have really focused the individual's contribution, with the minimum of paperwork.

Individual development/action plans

Although individual development plans are not specifically required for Investors in People, they can be very effective in setting down individual contributions to the business, and linking them to training and development activities. The example given in Figure 15 would also help to satisfy the requirements of Indicator 2.3.

Sample individual development plan			
Name: Margaret Jones		**Line manager:** Aileen Smart **Date Agreed:** 10 October 1995 **Date for Review:** 10 March 1996	
Area of activity	Target/standard	Method	To be achieved by (date)
Machine running	To increase throughput to 250 units per hour at existing level of quality	Supervised practice (with Jean Peters)	30/11/95
Health and safety in machine cleaning	To be able to fully comply with Health and Safety operating procedure No. 12/95	1. Attend briefing seminar, in house 2. Supervised practice/ demonstration	30/11/95 31/12/95
New feed system	To achieve 90 per cent utilization of new system and equipment	On-job instruction (with Jean) and practice	When new plant installed (by 31/3/96 at latest)

Figure 15   Sample individual development plan: individual development or action plans can be very helpful in setting specific targets or standards for development activities

You will see that it combines operational targets and training/development targets. I have seen some very good examples of this approach. The main benefit of doing it this way is that it helps promote the understanding that training and development should contribute to the achievement of operational/business objectives.

Note the specific nature of the targets or standards. Far too many training/development actions are undertaken without clear targets or standards to be achieved. The more specific you can be, the easier it will be to satisfy Indicator 2.6, and evaluate your training and development activities under Principle 4. We will pick this theme up again when we look at Indicator 2.6.

But there's more

Investors in People offers such a powerful opportunity to enhance your business. Consider this:

Research by management consultants Touche Ross in 1990–91 shows that about 45 per cent of new business ideas come from employees and customers. Incidentally, 15 per cent of new business ideas come from managing directors, and about 3 per cent from consultants. Does anybody listen to the van drivers, the carpet fitters, the service engineers, when they come back and say 'Mrs Bloggs the customer was asking if we could do it in blue with bells on'? Would they think to report such a request anyway? Have you asked them?

Who knows best how to change the job to make it more efficient, more effective, to improve quality? The person doing it, usually. Many a time and motion or ergonomics expert has been upstaged by an old hand who has been doing the job for years.

Would you be interested in a 5 per cent efficiency gain here, a 10 per cent reduction in wastage there? I bet you would. Why on earth don't you ask the people doing the job? If you set the right climate, and ask them in the right way, they will tell you – believe me.

Taking this idea a step further, why not bring together a cross-functional team of people to look for efficiency gains or solve problems in specific areas of your operations?

Many organizations do this, with considerable benefit to the business and a clear demonstration to the workforce that their ideas are taken seriously. If you take this route, here are a few important points to bear in mind:

- No idea should be discounted, until the group has considered it fully. Avoid flashlamp thinking (seeing only the obvious, and ignoring the lateral possibilities);
- The group should have direct access to the top of the house. There needs to be a clear agreement that any idea sifted by the group and put to the chief executive merits serious consideration;

- Give the group limited financial authority to put its ideas into effect. In one small company its group is allowed to spend up to £100 on any one idea, without higher authority. Anything else goes up to the managing director.

I was working in a brewery some time ago. I talked to a wide range of people, from the executive team right through to the people who brew and deliver the beer. Among the most intelligent people I spoke to were a couple of draymen. What these two men didn't know about customer care was not worth knowing. They told me that, regardless of what other people in the company did, *they* were at the front line when it came to doing it right for the customer. But, they told me, when they brought back customer comments, no one in the brewery seemed to listen. I didn't need to check that. Their perception was, for them, reality.

Checking their brains in at the gate

Do all your people check their brains in at the gate when they come to work in the morning? I posed this question to a senior executive recently. 'Oh yes', he said, 'it's our company rule!' I think – I hope – he was joking.

'The Mexican Stand-off'

Investors in People is about communicating, as much as anything else. Do you share information with your people? Do they share with you? With each other? Is yours the kind of organization where the production people talk to the sales people, where accounts talk to customer care, where information flows freely up, down and sideways with the common aim of keeping the customer satisfied? Or is it just one great big Mexican stand-off, with each department or individual waiting to see who will make the first move?

The inverted pyramid

Some organizations become successful by turning the traditional approach to management right over on its head. In this kind of organization, the chief executive and board support the managers, who support the supervisors, who support the people doing the job. This can be represented by the inverted pyramid as shown in Figure 16.

Note who comes right at the top. The customer – with the employee right behind. Internal customers are of course employees anyway. The importance of closeness between customer and employee is appreciated and exploited by most successful organizations. Note also the term

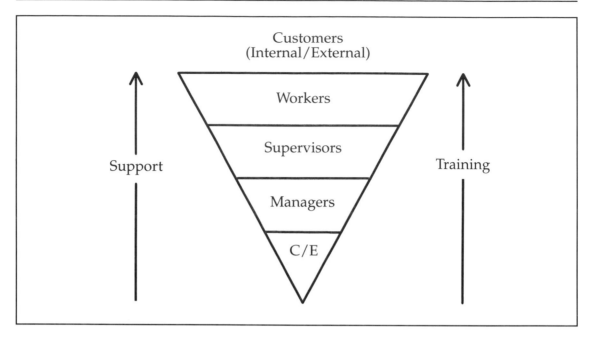

Figure 16   The inverted pyramid

'internal customer'. This will need no explanation to some readers – the sort of organization where sales, production, finance, engineering, and so on generally manage to pull together. If you do not use this concept in your organization, I suggest you give it serious consideration. It simply means treating colleagues with the same degree of respect you would afford customers, on the basis that they are not an inconvenience, but an essential part of the business.

You may be aware of the trend towards eliminating the pyramid in any form, in favour of flatter structures and 'matrix management'. It is up to you what management structure and style of operation you adopt. Whatever you choose the concept of empowering people to make your business better should not be ignored.

These are only concepts, and you have to ask yourself how they would work in your organization. Do not short change yourself by rejecting them out of hand. They work in one way or another for many organizations. The important point is how to help your people get better at what they do – for your good and for theirs.

Temperature check ✓

	YES	NO
A visitor to our organization would be impressed by the quality of thinking our people bring to the job.	☐	☐
We seldom experience confusion over who does what.	☐	☐
Our employees are always bringing us ideas to improve the business.	☐	☐
We always give these ideas serious thought and feed the results back to employees.	☐	☐
We have an active system for getting customers' views, through our employees.	☐	☐
Our customers see our employees as our greatest asset.	☐	☐

WHAT ACTION DO YOU NEED TO TAKE?

Indicator 1.6 *Where representative structures exist, management communicates with employee representatives a vision of where the organization is going and the contribution employees (and their representatives) will make to its success*

This Indicator applies to any organization where there is a structure for employee representation, either through trades unions or some other arrangement. The advice that follows is couched in terms of trade union representation, but the same principles apply in non-unionized environments.

53

The standard does not require you to set up representative structures where they do not already exist.

The Trades Union Congress has endorsed Investors in People, and you might infer from this that members and officials are expected to give it their support. How this works in practice will, of course, depend very much on the sort of relationship you have with your trades unions. Over the last couple of decades – even during times of what some would call trades union excess – I have met a fair number of union representatives who seemed to me a lot smarter than the company managers.

In some organizations the shop stewards' convenor is a member of the Investors in People steering group, and plays a very positive part in the process. In others they are struggling to come to terms with the very notion of having to sit down with the trade union in all but the most minimal and formal ways.

How to do it

This Indicator simply requires you to communicate with employee representatives a vision of where the organization is going, and the contribution employees, and their representatives will make to its success.

You may choose to do this as part of your existing consultative procedures with the unions, through specially arranged meetings or other communications with them. The standard does not say how often you should do this, but I would not be convinced this had been covered effectively where the organization had simply told the unions about its commitment to Investors in People, and left it at that.

I would expect to see some form of regular communication on the future of the organization and the wider subject of training and development. Bear in mind that:

- The requirements of this Indicator are over and above normal communications with your employees;
- The intention is to emphasize the two-way nature of training and development responsibilities. The organization has primary responsibility of course. But as emphasized elsewhere in this book, a balance has to be struck where the employee takes 'ownership' of training and development needs and how they will be met with the active support of the organization, through its managers.
- Involvement of your trade union representatives can help to establish the credibility of training and development strategy and actions.

Temperature check ✓

	YES	NO
The employee representatives in this organization play an important role in endorsing our training and development efforts.	☐	☐
Employee representatives are generally positive about our training and development activities.	☐	☐
We communicate regularly and effectively with employee representatives about the future direction of the organization.	☐	☐
Employee representatives are clear as to what they, and the workforce in general, are expected to contribute to the future of the business.	☐	☐

WHAT ACTION DO YOU NEED TO TAKE?

5 Planning

> **An Investor in People regularly reviews the training and development needs of all employees.**
>
> ● The resources for training and developing employees should be clearly identified in the business plan.
>
> ● Managers should be responsible for regularly agreeing training and development needs with each employee in the context of business objectives, setting targets and standards linked, where appropriate, to the achievement of National Vocational Qualifications (or relevant units), and in Scotland, Scottish Vocational Qualifications.

Indicator 2.1 *The written plan identifies the resources that will be used to meet training and development needs*

You need to have a training budget, separately identified in the written plan. There are two reasons for this.

1. It is of course a resource from which training and development activities can be funded.
2. Once training and development occupies its own line in the budget, it focuses management attention on the training and development effort. The same effect will not be achieved by hiding the training budget under 'office admin. etc.' – where it is often found. Why hide it there, for heaven's sake, if you accept its strategic importance to the business?

'Zero-based' budgeting

The training and development budget should be 'zero based'. In other words, it should be built up from needs identified in line with the business objectives. Contrast that with the well known company I visited recently. I asked the personnel director how the training budget was arrived at. She told me she took last year's figure, and added 5 per cent for inflation, plus 5 per cent to compensate for the reduction the board would make when they approved it.

Does this sound familiar? It is just as well the person concerned is someone who the board can trust to spend the company's money to good effect. But it is also easy to see how money can be spent unwisely and why training is still too frequently the first thing to be cut back in hard times, because senior management does not understand the broad costs and the returns available on their investment.

How to do it

Remember that money is not the only resource you might allocate to training and development. Don't forget to estimate:

● The amount of management time involved in supporting learners;
● The time of individual employees while they are trained on the job or away on courses etc;
● The cost of training facilities such as a resource centre or training materials.

It may be difficult to put a financial value on these, but make a rough estimate of the average amount of time spent by people on training and development in a year, and the average amount of management time spent on supporting that training. If you have internal trainers or workplace assessors, try to put a cost on the amount of time they bring to the equation.

The total may surprise you. Now, if you were spending that kind of money on new equipment, or on promotional literature, wouldn't you make sure you got exactly what you needed? So why do so many organizations adopt a hit and miss approach to training? Don't they want value for money?

Although I have emphasized the importance of zero-based budgeting, it can be helpful to express your estimate in relative terms – for example as a percentage of sales turnover or payroll, or as a notional average days of training per employee over the year. Relative figures like this can help everyone – particularly managers – to get a feel for the amount invested, and think about training and development in value-for-money terms.

Temperature check ✓

	YES	NO
People in this organization are fully aware of the resources available for training and development.	☐	☐
We have a training and development budget which is zero-based (that is based on needs).	☐	☐
Our employees know about the resources available for their development.	☐	☐
Our budget and resources are adequate to meet the needs we have identified.	☐	☐
We review our training/development budget every time we review our business objectives.	☐	☐

WHAT ACTION DO YOU NEED TO TAKE?

Indicator 2.2 *Training and development needs are regularly reviewed against business objectives*

This assumes that you regularly review the business objectives themselves. How often do you do this? At quarterly reviews? At monthly board meetings? At weekly team meetings? How good are you at monitoring the external environment and its effect on the business objectives?

How to do it

Remember the model we looked at earlier for monitoring the external environment (page 00)? Do you apply such a model to your business? Does it lead you on to consider the technological and process implications for your business? You must, surely.

Looking beyond that, if you accept the proposition made earlier that most businesses are technology constrained – there is a limit to the gains you can make from technology alone – what are you going to do about the training and development implications of these external forces?

Is profitability a standing item on your board meeting agenda? Is cash flow? Is profit centre performance? I bet they are. Then get training and development on the agenda too – and at management/team meetings right down the line. Make sure it is near the top of the agenda, not the last item which will be skimped or dropped if the meeting runs out of time. It is far too important for that.

Temperature check ✓

	YES	NO
Directors and senior managers review the business goals regularly enough to keep us ahead of the competition.	☐	☐
We expect all our people to help us monitor external forces that will affect our business plans.	☐	☐
We involve all our people in reviewing the business.	☐	☐
Training and development is a standing item at board and team meetings.	☐	☐

WHAT ACTION DO YOU NEED TO TAKE?

Indicator 2.3 *A process exists for regularly reviewing the training and development needs of all employees*

How often do you sit down with your people to discuss their training and development needs in relation to the job and the company's future? You really do need to have some kind of system for this, even in the smallest organization.

It could be a full blown employee appraisal system, or something much simpler for a small organization. You do not need to have this in writing for Investors in People, but how are you going to keep track of what training needs have been identified, what action has been agreed, and what progress has been made, if you don't have some way of recording it?

How to do it

Realistically, you need some sort of system that deals with the following questions:

- Since the last review, how well has the employee performed against the main requirements of the job?
- What areas does this throw up for development in the next period?
- What changes to the business objectives, or other internal/external factors, will cause the employee to need further training and development during the coming period?
- How can these needs be met in the most cost-effective way?
- How will these be translated into action for the individual and at team/organization level?
- How will you measure the outcomes?

An outline of a simple review document is given in Figure 17. You could be much more elaborate if you feel it would add value to your business.

Temperature check ✓

	YES	NO
Managers in this organization are good at identifying where their people need to develop.	☐	☐
I could find out immediately what the main training and development needs of our people are by checking our system or asking managers.	☐	☐
The system is easy to use, and understood by everyone.	☐	☐
The system works for everyone, in every department.	☐	☐

WHAT ACTION DO YOU NEED TO TAKE?

Training and Development Review

Name:	Time in Job:	yrs/months
Job Title:	Last Review (date):	
Department:	Next Review due (date):	

1. What are the main tasks in your job (from your job description)?

2. What are the main competences required (from your job description)?

3. What changes do you foresee in your job over the period to the next training and development review?

4. What training/development would help you to develop the competences required for your job?

5. How could this be organized?

Training and development needs/actions agreed.

Signed (Job Holder) . . . . Date . . . .

(Manager). . . . . Date . . . .

Figure 17   Sample training and development review form

Indicator 2.4 *Responsibility for developing people is clearly identified throughout the organization, starting at the top*

The actions you take to demonstrate commitment (Indicator 1.1) should show clearly that the top executive in your organization is committed to the development of people. This Indicator is to do with how that responsibility cascades down the organization.

In a trial assessment of a small organization I carried out recently, they had just completed an employee survey on all aspects of training and development. Well over 90 per cent of the workforce said they would ask their manager if they needed any help or advice on their development. This organization had taken very simple but effective steps to make sure everyone recognized the managers' role. Some of these are touched on below.

How to do it

The training and development role of managers and supervisors can be expressed in a number of ways, including:

- A statement to all employees, perhaps as an extract of the business plan or training policy;
- Writing it into all managers' job descriptions;
- Monitoring their performance in this area;
- Making managers highly visible in the process – for example making sure they discuss training and development at all their team meetings;
- Posting notices setting out the role of the manager in training and development (probably as part of a statement about your commitment);
- Having managers report up formally on training and development activities on a frequent basis, at least quarterly.

You can do any or all of these. I suggest you write it into managers' job descriptions as a minimum – and then assess their performance on this, as you would with any other aspect of their work.

Temperature check ✓

	YES	NO
Our directors/senior managers understand the importance of line managers in developing our business through developing people.	☐	☐
All employees are clear on the manager's role in training and development.	☐	☐
If an assessor spoke to our managers today, they would give a clear account of their role in training and development.	☐	☐
We take effective action to support line managers in this critical area.	☐	☐

WHAT ACTION DO YOU NEED TO TAKE?

Indicator 2.5 *Managers are competent to carry out their responsibilities for developing people*

It is foolish to expect managers to take responsibility for training and developing their people without ensuring that they are competent to carry it out effectively. Do not assume that managers will know how to do it.

Most managers – particularly at junior and middle levels – came straight from the shop floor. They suddenly found themselves appointed to positions as supervisors or managers, without training of any sort. It was simply assumed that, because they were good at their job, they would make good managers. The usual outcome of this, as many people have found to their cost, is that the organization loses a good 'worker' and gains a lousy manager. Much worse, the effect is magnified on employees as the manager blunders around firing off orders because he/she thinks that is what being a manager involves. It is no wonder that so many people do not give a hoot about the standard of work they produce. It is no surprise that so many quality initiatives fail, because managers have not created a climate in which people will think for themselves.

Them and us

The situation worsens the higher up the professional ladder you go. In many of the higher levels of profession, the subject of the manager's or professional's role in training and development is given scant consideration (although it is getting better through the efforts of some of the professional institutions). I am sure we have all met solicitors, doctors, accountants and civil engineers who have no idea how to talk to their people. They seem to assume that, because they are stars in their particular firmament, they always know better than their employees. In many cases this will, of course, be true. But in many other instances, it is nothing more than professional arrogance.

It is no wonder we have a 'them and us' problem in so many organizations. I was working recently with a world-renowned luxury goods manufacturer. This company operates in an extremely competitive environment, where individual contributions could make the difference between success and failure. Despite valiant attempts by the HR department to interest the workforce in quality, most of the people I spoke to didn't seem to care too much. The most frequent comment from the people I spoke to was that the company directors would pass them on the shop floor without so much as acknowledging their existence.

How can you expect people to go the extra mile if you treat them like that? Investors in People is not about being nice to people, but you will hardly get the best from it without some of the basic courtesies.

The great tragedy of all this is that the investment needed to make directors and managers effective in this important area of developing people is comparatively low. A couple of days basic management training would at least be a start. I am pleased to say that some organizations take a much more enlightened view. Perhaps that includes your competitors.

How to do it

Train your managers

Assuming they at least know how to talk to their people, your managers should also be able to:

- Help them understand what the business is about;
- Help them understand what they are expected to contribute;
- Help individuals identify their training and development needs;
- Understand the benefits of training and development – for the organization and the individual;
- Understand why and how people learn/what makes them tick;

- Identify the main options for meeting training and development needs;
- Coach and support the individual learner;
- Agree training targets and standards;
- Evaluate training and development actions.

Do not assume they can do this. It will not cost very much to bring your managers up to a basic level of competence in these areas. I have run numerous one- and two-day workshop programmes through which managers have at least had their eyes opened, at least enough to let in some light.

I was running such a workshop for a public sector body a few months back. The training manager told me that one of the supervisors present had the reputation of bullying his staff, but did not seem capable of recognizing or doing anything about it. By the end of the two-day workshop, the supervisor was cracking jokes at his own expense about his poor approach to staff. He and his team have since been involved in a team development programme, with the training manager's help, and the signs of recovery are good.

It is worth mentioning that the senior manager in this case took a direct interest and supported the supervisor's new approach to team development. The fact that she was on a similar workshop around the same time might have influenced matters. It underlines yet again the importance of management support at all levels.

Managers can learn a great deal in the kind of workshop or seminar described above, but you should beware of looking for 'quick fixes' in developing your managers in this key area of responsibility. Developing management skills is an ongoing process, and building it into your business development process is an integral part of Investors in People.

Temperature check ✓

	YES	NO
Our managers see training and development as an integral aspect of the business.	☐	☐
Our managers know how to help their people get access to appropriate training and development opportunities.	☐	☐
Our managers are good at encouraging individual development for the benefit of the business.	☐	☐

WHAT ACTION DO YOU NEED TO TAKE?

Indicator 2.6 *Targets and standards are set for development actions*

Indicator 2.7 *Where appropriate, training targets are linked to achieving external standards, and particularly to National Vocational Qualifications (or Scottish Vocational Qualifications in Scotland) and units.*

I will deal with these two Indicators together, as their intent is broadly similar.

First of all, let us clarify why we need to have targets and standards for training and development:

1. You will find it difficult to evaluate the effects of training and development, if you have not agreed a target or standard with the learner, before the development activity takes place. How will you know if you've arrived at your destination, if you did not know where you were trying to get to in the first place?
2. It is often better to use external standards as a benchmark. This is increasingly important in demonstrating to customers that your employees' standards of competence are at or above the level expected in your industry sector. Perhaps your competitors are already doing this.

How to do it

There are several ways of adopting or developing targets and standards for development actions:

- You can devise your own;
- You can adopt industry standards;
- You can adopt the standards set by key customers;
- You can introduce vocational qualifications – National Vocational Qualifications (NVQs), Scottish Vocational Qualifications (SVQs), or units towards them.

Agreeing targets and standards

You should agree with the learner:

- What the learner should be able to do once the development activity has been carried out;
- To what standard of performance.

These are equally important, because they enable both learner and manager to measure the effectiveness of the development activity itself and changes in the learner's performance against the required standard.

Examples of targets and standards

Word processing provides a commonly understood vehicle for demonstrating how development targets and standards can be framed:

'to be able to use Microsoft Word for processing reports, memos, and letters [the target] . . . in accordance with the company's approved corporate style [the standard]'.

Consider these further examples. Can you identify the target for each? Can you then identify the standard for each one?

1. 'To be able to use the photocopier in accordance with the procedures set out in the operating manual';
2. 'To be able to take incoming telephone calls and transfer them';
3. 'To develop competence in considering and deciding applications for rebate';
4. 'To be capable of setting up and running the press at the rate of 200 units per minute, with a rejection rate of less than 1 per cent';
5. 'To be able to write business letters'.

Are these all targets and standards as described above? Or are some of them only partly complete? Examples 2 and 3 are incomplete, because they do not set standards. The telephone handling example might have referred to standards on speed of response (for example answering incoming calls within three rings) or the organization's house-style (for example 'good morning, XYZ Optical Equipment Limited, Jeff speaking', and so on).

Example 3 could refer to the organization's published policy on rebates. But what about example 5 – writing business letters? Is this a standard? I would say not, as business letters can mean different things to different people. It would be much better to link the objective to a standard such as 'according to our normal house style' or relate it to a recognized vocational qualification in business letter writing.

Targets and standards cannot always be stated in measurable terms, but isn't example 4 a good way of setting an objective against which we can measure the learner's progress?

Relating learning objectives/standards to specific actions

Once the means of meeting the need has been identified, the target/standard can then be expressed in terms of what that specific activity should achieve. Take, for example, the photocopying example given above. The target and standard for the specific learning activity might be expressed as:

'by the end of the practical instruction, the learner will be able to use the photocopier in accordance with the procedures set out in the operating manual'.

So, the target and standard remain the same. All we have done is to link them to a specific activity, in this case a practical instruction session. The key thing is that we have set an objective against which progress can be assessed. At the end of the practical instruction session in this case, we can ask the question 'can the learner do it or not?' and take whatever additional action is needed.

Temperature check ✓

	YES	NO
We know how to set targets and standards for individual training and development activities.	☐	☐
We know what external standards apply to our areas of work.	☐	☐
Managers are able to help their people to set targets and standards.	☐	☐
Our people understand the link between targets, standards and evaluation.	☐	☐
Employees are supported in working to external standards including NVQs/SVQs appropriate to the job.	☐	☐

WHAT ACTION DO YOU NEED TO TAKE?

---

6 Action

An Investor in People takes action to train and
develop individuals on recruitment and
throughout their employment.

- Action should focus on the training needs of all new recruits and
continually developing and improving the skills of existing
employees.

- All employees should be encouraged to contribute to identifying and meeting their own job-related development needs.

Indicator 3.1 *All new employees are introduced effectively to the organization and are given the training and development they need to do their jobs*

Did you ever start a job, perhaps on a wet Monday in March, and
nobody knew you were coming? Fun, isn't it!

If it has not happened to you, is it possible that you might have been
guilty of doing it to someone else? Maybe you forgot, or one of your
colleagues was supposed to do it in your absence on holiday, or you
were called away on urgent business, and so on. Whether you have a
good reason or just an excuse for failing in the employee's induction,
there are two immediate outcomes:

1. The new recruit is left feeling like a spare part, and probably
wondering whether they did the right thing in accepting the job.
No matter how much they manage to force a smile, they will

always remember their first day in your organization. You have got off to what might be termed an 'inauspicious start';

2. You can imagine the conversation round the dinner table or down at the pub, when people ask 'How's the new job, John?' 'Oh all right ... I think. Mind you they're a hopeless lot. Left me standing around for nearly two hours while they figured out what to do with me. They forgot I was coming.'

Not very good for your image, is it? To be honest, you look a complete fool – and you probably deserve it.

How to do it

Develop an induction programme

You owe it to yourself and your new recruit to have a structured induction programme, setting out clear responsibilities for its effective implementation. You should have contingency arrangements to make sure it operates regardless of absences or operational difficulties. Nothing less will do.

If you are not convinced of the need for effective induction, ask yourself:

● What damage could the newcomer do to your image or to customer goodwill if you do not start the induction programme immediately?

● What damage could they do to themselves or others?

● Do you want to play Russian Roulette with your image and your new employee's commitment by letting them loose without at least some idea of what they are doing?

I have seen some excellent induction systems. It doesn't have to be cumbersome. For example, one organization starts its induction programme early on in the recruitment phase. When shortlisted candidates are invited for interview, they receive a copy of the mission statement and a summary of the organization's goals. This employer believes it gives candidates a fairer chance to shine at the interview, by letting them know something of the organization they might be coming to work for. It is also an important opportunity to emphasize how professional the company is in its approach to people.

The key components and features of this particular system are:

● Responsibility rests firmly with managers/team leaders, who are expected to genuinely welcome the newcomer into the organization;

- Responsibilities are set out clearly and managers/team leaders understand them;
- There is a simple checklist of things to be covered;
- The system is evaluated every time it is used, using a short questionnaire which is completed by the individual and the team leader. New employees are therefore closely involved in the evaluation, and this emphasizes from the outset that they are also responsible for taking an active role in their own development.

Now, surely that has to be a better approach than leaving newcomers twiddling their thumbs for the first couple of hours – because you forgot they were coming. Never mind Investors in People – it just makes sense!

Easy to do, and immediate benefits

The beauty of effective induction is that, like many development activities, it is very easy to do, and it repays you immediately. The time taken to do it properly will be no more – and maybe much less – than the time you might have to spend undoing the newcomer's mistakes if you failed to explain things properly in the first place. More to the point, the new employee is made to feel welcome, part of the team, straight away.

Ask yourself this. If a key customer was planning to pay you a visit, would you make that person feel unwelcome and uncomfortable? Presumably not. So why would you leave it to chance with a new, and valued, member of the team?

Remember that induction is about more than where the toilets are and the name of the person working next door. Use the checklist in Figure 18 and add to it, to develop your own induction programme. Why not involve your managers and other employees in developing the induction checklist? Who better to know what needs to be covered than the people doing the job?

Two further points on induction:

- Don't try to deliver it all at once. The new recruit will never take it all in. Cover the things that the new employee must know within the first hour or two – for example key safety or hygiene rules, the mission and goals of the organization, and so on (I call this the 'survival kit'). Then make the induction a gradual process over the next two or three days. Design your induction checklist to allow for this. My sample checklist (Figure 18) refers to Stage 1 and Stage 2 induction, but you can structure it any way you want, depending on the needs of your organization. Just make sure it is effective.
- Evaluate it every time you use it. Involve new employees in evaluating the process:

Induction Checklist

Name of Employee:.. Start Date:..................

Line Manager: ....

STAGE 1 INDUCTION – ORGANIZATION LEVEL

Subject	Activity	Responsibility	Completed Date/Signatures
Mission and objectives	Issue and discuss	Personnel administrator	.... Employee .... P/Admin
Key health and safety rules	Issue and discuss	Personnel administrator	.... Employee .... P/Admin
Personnel/ disciplinary matters	Issue employee handbook and discuss	Personnel administrator	.... Employee .... P/Admin
Training and development policy	Issue and discuss	Personnel administrator	.... Employee .... P/Admin
Key personnel and department functions	Issue/explain organization chart	Personnel administrator	.... Employee .... P/Admin

Immediate colleagues	Introduce personally	Personnel administrator	.... Employee .... P/Admin
Handover to line manager	Introduce personally	Personnel administrator and line manager	.... Employee .... P/Admin

STAGE 2 INDUCTION – DEPARTMENT LEVEL

Clothing and personal equipment	Ensure immediate issue	Line manager	.... Employee .... Manager
Main areas of department operations	Tour of area and explain	Line manager	.... Employee .... Manager
Health and safety	Explain main hazards and precautions	Line manager	.... Employee .... Manager
	Point out H&S notices and procedures	Line manager	.... Employee .... Manager
	Issue departmental instructions	Line manager	.... Employee .... Manager

Figure 18   Sample induction checklist. Use this to prepare one that suits your organization.

– observe and question them
– have them explain the key points back to you
– have them sign off the various elements, as shown in Figure 18.

You can also have the line manager complete a ticklist of all the main elements, giving his or her view of how well the employee has understood. This has the added benefit of emphasizing to the line manager that he or she is responsible for the newcomer.

Temperature check ✓

	YES	NO
Our induction programme is a showcase for the organization.	☐	☐
We make new people feel part of the team from the moment they arrive.	☐	☐
Managers are clear on their role in induction.	☐	☐
We check on the effectiveness of our induction every time it is used.	☐	☐
Our induction programme is also used for people transferring between departments or teams.	☐	☐

WHAT ACTION DO YOU NEED TO TAKE?

Indicator 3.2 *The skills of existing employees are developed in line with business objectives*

Your approach to this Indicator should integrate with your approach to a number of others. You may remember that:

● Your business plan needs to highlight broad development needs (Indicator 1.4);
● Training and development needs must be regularly reviewed against business objectives (Indicator 2.2); and
● A process must exist for regularly reviewing the training and development needs of employees (Indicator 2.3).

How to do it

To meet the national standard, you will have to produce evidence to show that you take an ongoing approach to developing your people. You will need to show how the processes link together, to ensure that employees can do their current jobs and that you look ahead to anticipate the needs arising from internal change, such as:

- Restructuring;
- The need for multiskilling;
- Developing people for promotion;
- Succession planning/contingency cover for key posts;
- Encouraging self-management and problem solving abilities.

Also consider external changes, as highlighted earlier. Use the SPLICET framework for environmental monitoring to help you consider external factors systematically.

Then look at some of the options for training and development set out under Indicator 3.3. Involve your employees in the process of deciding how to meet their needs, as discussed under Indicator 3.4.

Temperature check ✓

	YES	NO
The development of our people is always uppermost in our minds when we review the business objectives.	☐	☐
Our employees are briefed and trained to cope with change.	☐	☐
Our employees understand that their development is ongoing in our changing world.	☐	☐
We have systems in place to ensure that people are developed to fill key posts if needed.	☐	☐

WHAT ACTION DO YOU NEED TO TAKE?

Indicator 3.3 *All employees are made aware of the development opportunities open to them*

Remember that Investors in People is not concerned with training alone. Nor is it just about the present. It involves taking a much broader look at how we can encourage the maximum contribution from the entire workforce. This means developing your business – through developing your people. Many organizations have discovered that by encouraging their people to take more responsibility – and of course by supporting them through training and development – they are able to take on the competition and win.

You cannot do that without opening up opportunities for your employees, and making them known to all. This does not mean that everyone will be off developing themselves all the time. There is a business to run, after all. But by using some thought and imagination, it is possible to see how cost-effective development opportunities can be made available to your employees, with tremendous potential pay-off to the business.

How to do it

Here are some of the more obvious options. I have put my five 'favourites' at the top of the list. These are generally the most cost-effective. You may be using others, and it would be useful to highlight them also as part of your portfolio of evidence.

- **Handing over responsibility.** This most basic form of developing people requires little or nothing by way of special equipment, absences from the workplace, or expense of any sort. What it does require – to work effectively – is an investment of time in instructing, supporting and coaching the learner, based on a clear definition of the standards to be achieved. 'Delegation', 'empowerment', 'inverted pyramid' whatever terminology you adopt, the 'secret' lies in driving down decision making to the lowest level. This is particularly difficult for managers and owners of expanding small businesses, because it involves giving up control over aspects of what is essentially 'their baby'. But remember that handing over responsibility can do wonders for the business, by freeing up management time for key business development activities.

- **Involvement in meetings,** product development meetings, market development and sales meetings, and so on. Try to focus your meetings on the future – what's happening next week, the plans for the next month, next year's targets, the 3–5 year strategy, and so on.
- **Working with experienced employees** – often referred to as 'sitting with Nellie'. Using experienced people is the natural way to approach many training and development needs. It can be highly effective, but only if you ensure that the experienced workers pass on the right information in a logical way. You might need to invest some time in having them trained in instructional techniques.
- **Face-to-face instruction, coaching, mentoring and counselling** – all related to the above approach. The same cautions apply. You need to pick your best people and make sure they know how to help the learner. Don't make the mistake that because someone has a nice way with people, they will be effective at this. It helps of course, but you need to invest in their skills, if this is going to work.
- **Individual work-related projects** – where the employee is asked to study a particular problem or opportunity for the organization. This can have several benefits, including solving the problem/opportunity, helping the individual to learn more about the particular topic, and developing self-reliance in the process.
- **Short courses** – run in house, or off site. These could be exclusively for your own personnel, or mixed programmes with delegates from other organizations. They can of course be run by your own people – why not use the in-house expertise at your fingertips.
- **Training and education programmes** – part-time, involving day-release or evening classes, or sponsoring an employee to take time out for full-time study.
- **Job swaps** – within our outwith the team, department, or branch.
- **Job rotation** – where individuals go through a programme of planned work experience, to give them a broader understanding of the organization and where various operations fit in.
- **Job shadowing** – a short period of time observing and learning from the work of a colleague.
- **Cross-functional project teams** – where people from different parts of the organization are brought together to tackle specific problems or opportunities.
- **Problem solving projects** with customers or suppliers.
- **Visits to customers, suppliers, and so on** – which can be very effective to help employees understand the job better, and also useful for building relationships with key contacts outside the organization.

- Longer-term **secondments**, to learn more about problems and opportunities common to your organization and your suppliers or customers.
- **Reading** – appropriate technical literature, handouts, notes and articles can all be helpful. But not too much of it. Few people like having to struggle through a great quantity of reading. You need to make sure the trainee understands it – back to evaluation yet again!
- **Video programmes** – 'traditional' video can be effective, but it is important to choose carefully to ensure relevance to the employee's job and to your organization. Make it less passive by briefing the trainee on what to look out for in the video, and discussing it with them afterwards. Watching the video twice can be very effective, as the viewer often misses some of the meaning first time around.
- **Interactive video** and CD Interactive (CDi) – highly effective ways of involving learners in simulated situations where they have to make decisions. The programme then confirms or challenges the decision made, giving reasons and reviewing the lessons learned. Can be expensive and likely to be affordable only for larger organizations. But there might be a chance of getting access through another company or a training or education organization.
- **Computer based training packages** – have some similarity with interactive video, because the trainee has to react to the problems and questions posed, and the software is programmed to feed back appropriate responses.
- **Flexible learning** – using bought-in packages of materials, which trainees work through at their own pace. They may be based on video, text, audio tapes, technical kits or a combination. There are very many packages available and, as you might expect, some are better than others.

Creative solutions

Often, the solution to training and development needs is a combination of the above methods. It is worth re-emphasizing that the activities have to be carefully planned. Do not throw learners a computer training programme, a flexible learning package, or a book, and expect them to learn on their own.

The process must be planned, managed and evaluated. Otherwise, you may well be wasting your time and the trainees'.

┌───┐

Temperature check ✓

                                                        YES NO

Our employees are supported to develop in line
with business objectives.   ☐   ☐

Our employees are aware of the main development
options open to them.   ☐   ☐

Managers and employees are aware of the variety of
routes to individual development, in line with business
objectives.   ☐   ☐

Everyone in our workforce is included in relevant
development activities.   ☐   ☐

WHAT ACTION DO YOU NEED TO TAKE?

└───┘

Indicator 3.4 *All employees are encouraged to help identify and meet their job-related development needs*

This Indicator challenges the notion of training and development being something that is done by someone to someone else. You may have been on a training course where half the delegates were there 'because they were sent'. What kind of basis is that for developing people?

Punishment or reward?

Is yours the sort of organization where training is used as a punishment?

'Jean's been really bad these last few months. I think we'd better send her on a course.'

or as a reward?

'Jean's been really good these last few months. I think we'd better send her on a course.'

How to do it

The key to success in developing people is to encourage them to take responsibility for their own learning – take charge of it. If you have any idea about developing people, you must realize that:

- They must know what the organization is aiming to do;
- They must know what is expected of them; and
- They must know how their performance will be measured.

So doesn't it make sense to delegate responsibility for identifying their own learning needs as well? And to make sure they do it effectively, why don't you sit down with them occasionally to ask for their views? Help them to think through the following:

- The world is changing – that means this organization, my job, what our customers expect, what the organization expects from me;
- The organization needs me to do my job as effectively as possible, so we can stay in business and hopefully grow;
- The organization will support me in doing that;
- So, what do I need and how can we deliver it jointly?

You need to do this once a year at the very least. Many organizations do it every six months, and others on a quarterly basis. They invest this

---

Temperature check ✓

	YES	NO
Reward and punishment are the basis of our training and development practices.	☐	☐
All our employees understand their responsibility for their own development, with our support.	☐	☐
Employees in this organization drive their own training and development.	☐	☐
We are good at supporting the training and development of employees.	☐	☐

WHAT ACTION DO YOU NEED TO TAKE?

time because they know it makes sound business sense to keep their employees focused on the way ahead and to help them identify and meet their development needs. The amount of time involved in doing a quarterly review with one individual is about three to four hours of the individual's time and three to four hours of the manager's time *in a year*. Hardly what you would call onerous is it?

Indicator 3.5 *Effective action takes place to achieve the training and development objectives of individuals and the organization*

Much of this has been dealt with in other sections of the book. It is worth emphasizing at this point that although, in Investors in People terms, training and development is primarily for the benefit of the organization, there is no reason why it should not also benefit the individual.

Many organizations approach the development of people in this broader way. Some of these organizations will support their employees' learning activities regardless of their relevance to the business plan. They do this because they believe that to encourage learning in its widest sense keeps people fresh, and enables them to adapt to the changing world of business. In other words, it brings an indirect benefit to the business. It is up to you to decide whether you could support this broader kind of development, and whether it would offer significant benefits to your organization.

This balancing of benefits to the organization and the individual can be expressed simply by two overlapping circles, as shown in Figure 19.

The more the two circles overlap, the better the fit between organizational and individual needs. Where does the balance of your training and development activities lie? Bear in mind that Investors in People emphasizes the need to develop people in line with the business objectives. But could your organization gain even more from looking at individual learning in this broader context?

How to do it

As stated earlier, much of the detail is covered in other Indicators, where I have emphasized the importance of:

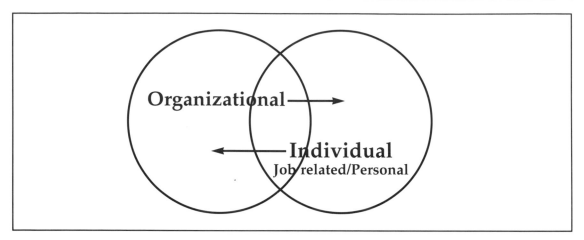

Figure 19 **Balancing organization and individual training/development needs. The more the two circles overlap, the better the fit between the needs of the organization and the individual. Individual needs may be directly relevant to the job or for broader personal development.**

- Starting off the way you should continue, through effective induction;
- Having sound business reasons for developing people;
- Making employees and managers aware of the wide range of options available for training and development;
- Encouraging individuals to take ownership of their own training and development.

Indicator 3.5 deals with making the whole of Principle 3 – 'Action' – work in practice. The emphasis is on effectiveness. The Assessor will want to see evidence that the systems you have put in place actually work, and that they link back to the needs of the business.

The acid test is applied when individuals are asked how the system works for them:

- Did the training review process they underwent produce agreed actions that were actually carried out? Or did their needs get lost somewhere along the way?
- Were they sent on a course, when in fact 'sitting with Nellie' would have suited them better?
- Did the line manager help them to make sense of the business objectives and relate their training and development activities to them?
- Were all employees considered as part of the process, or was someone in the furthest outpost missed out?

Temperature check ✓

	YES	NO
We achieve a good balance of organizational and individual benefit from training and development.	☐	☐
Our training and development activities are usually effective in helping us achieve our business objectives.	☐	☐
If the assessor asked our people today, they would testify to the effectiveness of our development actions.	☐	☐

WHAT ACTION DO YOU NEED TO TAKE?

Indicator 3.6 *Managers are actively involved in supporting employees to meet their training and development needs*

I once had a boss who took great exception to the fact that I had been selected for an in-house management development programme. I was about half-way through the programme when I suddenly found myself transferred into his department. This meant he inherited the programme along with me. He made it clear from the outset that 'in my day we didn't have anything like this', and he couldn't see the need for it. Far from supporting me, he poured scorn on my endeavours. What really hacked me off was when he marked the days I was scheduled to attend tutorials on his wall planner – in red ink. Only after much discussion was I able to bring him round to seeing the point of this training.

An extreme, but not untypical example. One of the questions I always ask people when I visit an organization is 'how much support do you get from your boss for your training and development?' This gives rise to the possibilities illustrated by Figure 20.

Where are your managers on that scale shown in Figure 20? Do they covertly or overtly oppose the development of your people? Are they active supporters? Or do they simply tolerate it? What signals does this send out to your employees?

You might be personally committed to Investors in People, but you cannot possibly make it work if you have not convinced – and trained – your managers to support their learners.

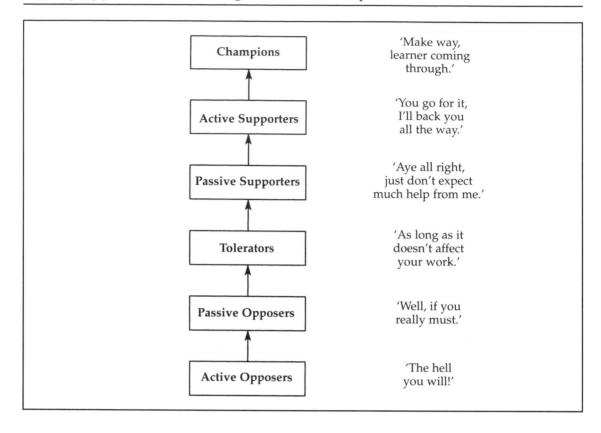

Figure 20   Degrees of managers' support/opposition for training and development. How do your managers perform?

How to do it

As we have already seen, managers need to be trained and developed themselves, if they are to carry out their responsibilities for developing their people. The point has also been made forcibly that these responsibilities need to be made clear to everyone in the organization, not least to the managers. Only by dealing effectively with these two issues can you develop a culture wherein managers will truly support their people in their development. You need to make sure they take this seriously, by having managers report up the line, as highlighted earlier.

Temperature check ✓

	YES	NO
Generally speaking, our managers are active supporters of individual learners.	☐	☐
We have identified any managers who are less than active in their support, and are working on them.	☐	☐
We train or brief all our managers to understand the importance of supporting learners.	☐	☐

WHAT ACTION DO YOU NEED TO TAKE?

7 Evaluation

An Investor in People evaluates the investment in training and development to assess achievement and improve future effectiveness.

- The investment, the competence and commitment of employees, and the use made of the skills learned should be reviewed at all levels against business goals and targets.

- The effectiveness of training and development should be reviewed at the top level and lead to renewed commitment and target setting.

Indicator 4.1 *The organization evaluates how its development of people is contributing to business goals and targets*

Indicator 4.2 *The organization evaluates whether its development actions have achieved their objectives*

Indicator 4.3 *The outcomes of training and development are evaluated at individual, team and organizational levels*

I will deal with these three Indicators together. That is not to diminish the importance of evaluation in any way, quite the opposite, in fact. It is in the way these three Indicators support each other, and how they link back to the business objectives, that Investors in People gathers much of its strength.

Put at its simplest, the standard requires you to evaluate:

- the effectiveness of your training and development activities in themselves – for example, if one of your employees attended a short course on credit control, did it achieve the targets or standards agreed under Indicator 2.6 or 2.7?
- The effect on individual performance – can the individual do the job better – in the credit control example, is the learner now able to reduce debtor days to the level you require?
- The impact on the team – what impact has the training had on immediate colleagues – for example, how much has the reduction in debtor days helped the finance department to achieve the objectives set for it within the business plan?
- The contribution to achieving your business objectives – if an improvement in the debtors' situation or in cashflow generally was not one of your objectives, why on earth did you spend money on debtor control training?

Your evaluation should, where appropriate, lead you to modify your approach to developing people in the light of your experience and in line with changes in the business. Not exactly brain surgery, is it?

This is an area many organizations have been avoiding for years, and it is easy to see why. Although the principles are hard to argue against, how do you evaluate the effect of training on your business objectives? How can you demonstrate cause and effect, given the numerous other factors that might influence the situation?

Can you genuinely say that the £1000 you spent on training your sales staff had an effect on the level of sales? What about the various other things that were happening at that time? The advertising and mailing campaign, for example. How do you know that it was the training rather than the campaign that produced the results? Or was it a combination of forces? You may never know with certainty. But you will certainly never know what contribution training made if you do not put a system in place to measure it.

How to do it

A simple evaluation loop, based on the relevant indicators, is given in Figure 21.

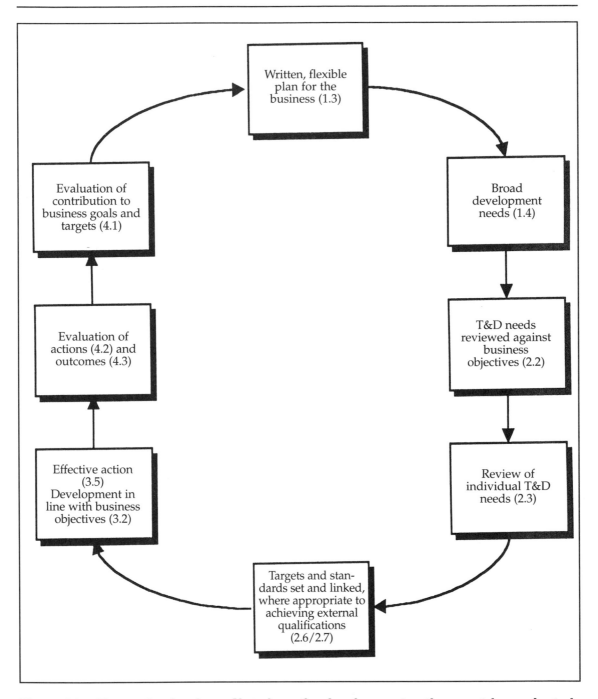

Figure 21   The evaluation loop. Note how the development action must be evaluated in terms of whether the action itself met the agreed objectives, and also in terms of its effect on the individual, the team and the organization. The contribution of training and development to the business objectives is an essential component of the evaluation process.

Evaluation – an example

Say, for example, that as part of your business plan, you are rolling out a new product line and have decided to mount a high volume direct mailing campaign. Among other things, you have identified a need for:

- Enhanced desk top publishing (DTP) skills to design low cost, attractive mailshots in-house;
- Improved telephone follow-up skills; and
- Detailed knowledge of the new product.

To meet these needs, you have assessed individual training and development needs, agreed targets and standards with the individuals who need the training, and have selected appropriate development activities. You have decided to:

- Ask your desk-top-publishing system supplier to take two of your people for a day each, for additional instruction on the system;
- Ask your senior sales executive to draft a telephone follow-up brief for the telesales team;
- Run a half day discussion/meeting with the administration team, to clarify their role and given them practice in using the brief;
- Run a practical demonstration of the new product and explain the benefits and key features to your sales team;
- Brief sales and order-taking staff on pricing, stocks, delivery, and introductory discounts.

Following the evaluation loop given in Figure 21, you should be able to measure, or at least make a broad assessment of, the effect of your training and development activities on:

- The speed, accuracy, and ability of the two people using the DTP system, by observation, discussion, and checking the sales literature they produce;
- The ability of the senior sales executive to produce a draft telesales brief, with support from you where necessary;
- The follow-up process, by observing admin staff using the brief, in 'role plays' during the practice session and also live, once the campaign has started;
- Staff understanding of the benefits, key features and other aspects of the new product.

At this point, you may be able to evaluate the learning activities and the outcomes. Taking the DTP training, did the day spent with the system supplier meet the targets and standards, and the learners' expectations?

Are the learners now capable of using the DTP system at a more advanced level?

The next thing to look at, of course, is the impact on the business.

- What has the direct mailing/telesales campaign achieved?
- Are the DTP'd materials working effectively as an introduction to potential customers?
- Are employees' new follow-up skills enabling them to convert leads to sales appointments?
- Are the sales people selling effectively? Is the new product line moving at the rate envisaged in the business plan?

So, the impact of the training and development can be measured through the success of the campaign itself. If you have run similar campaigns before, you should be able to compare the hit rates and form a view of how training and development has contributed to enhanced effectiveness.

There are many more measures of training effectiveness to be obtained from business performance than is generally realized. Obvious examples include:

- quality, working to tolerance, rejection, non-conformance and rework rates;
- service and delivery levels;
- returns from customers;
- complaints and so on.

It should be possible to measure or at least broadly assess the contribution of training and development to improvements in these areas.

Let me end with an example of how training can be evaluated without people being conscious of it. A colleague was discussing the benefits of training with the MD of a small company in glassware distribution. When he asked how the company evaluated training, the MD looked blank. As they were crossing the yard, they saw one of the employees loading a van with finished products. The MD made a passing comment that they used to be plagued by breakages, until (yes, you've guessed it) they trained the warehouse staff in improved handling techniques. They had since managed to reduce the level of breakages to such an extent that their insurers had lowered their insurance premiums.

How much evaluation are you doing without realizing it?

The manager's role in evaluation

As with the rest of the training and development process, the manager has a key role to play. It is simply not enough to have employees complete a course assessment form or similar document (usually known as a 'happy sheet'). This kind of evaluation does have some benefit – at least in spotting any significant mismatches between the training need and the method used to meet it. But given that 90 per cent of people in the UK do not normally complain if they receive poor service, the 'happy sheet' approach has to be taken with a pinch of salt.

The manager really needs to sit down with employees when they return from a training/development activity and discuss its effectiveness, using the evaluation loop outlined earlier, or something like it. Encourage employees to think about:

- The success of the event itself;
- The achievement of the targets and standards agreed beforehand;
- Their ability to apply the learning to the job;
- What further practice and support they will need.

Involving senior management in evaluation

It is key to the Investors in People process that managers right up the line should be involved in the evaluation of training and development. There are a number of aspects to this:

- I recommended earlier (in Indicator 2.4) that managers should be required to report up the line on training and development, on a regular basis. Evaluation should form an integral part of that reporting.
- Discussion of training and development at board and management meetings should include significant activities undertaken and the business results achieved from them.
- Senior managers should be encouraged to discuss the results of training and development activities with employees. I gave the example earlier of an organization where the directors have been given a target of talking to three or four people per month at random, to check the effectiveness of their communications. A similar approach could be taken to other training and development activities.
- If training and development responsibility is written into managers' job descriptions, their performance in evaluating it should be discussed at their own reviews.

Temperature check ✓

	YES	NO
We evaluate how our training and development activities contribute to achieving our business goals.	☐	☐
We evaluate our training and development activities against the targets and standards set for them.	☐	☐
We evaluate the impact of training and development activities on the individual, team and organization.	☐	☐
Our managers realize the importance of evaluating training and development activities against business objectives.	☐	☐

WHAT ACTION DO YOU NEED TO TAKE?

Indicator 4.4 *Top management understand the broad costs and benefits of developing people*

It is clear that commitment to developing people in line with the business objectives must come right from the top of the organization. This is, of course, a prime requirement of Investors in People. Equally important, it is vital if your employees are to be convinced on how seriously you take their development and their contribution to the business.

But, in order to feel able to continue making that commitment, top management must develop an understanding of the organization's training and development activities, in broad terms. Senior managers need to know that:

● Managers down the line are monitoring training and development expenditure – including time – in much the same way as they would monitor other expenditure against agreed budgets;
● A system is in place for ensuring that the investment is repaid in terms of increased efficiency, and so on, and potential impact on the business objectives.

95

In organizations where the concept of developing people to develop the business is well embedded – including many that were doing it long before Investors in People appeared – this process of assessing value for money from training is as natural as assessing performance in any part of the business.

In fact, when you talk to senior managers from these organizations, it is hard to believe that others adopt such a cavalier approach. I have had many stimulating discussions with senior managers in organizations where it is clear that training and development is highly valued – because they have seen what it can do for the business.

This brings me to two conclusions:

1.   It is only a matter of time before organizations that do not see the tangible business benefits of training and development are exposed as dinosaurs, to be consigned in time to the evolutionary scrap heap. It will take more time than some of us would like, but the behaviour and attitudes of these organizations are undoubtedly becoming unfashionable.
2.   Those managers who do not bother to consider the cost-benefit aspects of training and development are possibly misled by the small amounts of money involved. I have already made the point that, properly thought out, training and development can be very 'cheap'. Ironically this plays into the hands of the less enlightened manager, who sees the spend on training and development as hardly worth considering. It is just not very glamorous when viewed against the likes of key capital projects. Of course, what these people are failing to recognize is the leverage or multiplier effect on employees. This needs no explanation to any manager who has experienced the added value that motivated people bring to the business.

How to do it

This has largely been covered under other Indicators. To summarize:

●   Report on training as regularly and as seriously as you would with any other major aspect of the business;
●   Make the reporting system transparent – make sure that managers know it is important, make sure that senior managers endorse this importance, and make sure that everyone in the organization knows that management sees it that way;
●   Put training and development at or near the top of the agenda for board meetings, management meetings, and team meetings;
●   Ensure that training and development is constantly related back to the business plan and objectives.

> ## Temperature check ✓
>
> | | YES | NO |
> |---|---|---|
> | Training and development is a natural part of our senior management vocabulary. | ☐ | ☐ |
> | Our chief executive often surprises me by speaking knowledgeably about training and development. | ☐ | ☐ |
> | If the assessors visited us today, they would be amazed at our directors' interest in training and development. | ☐ | ☐ |
> | We are well attuned to obtaining value for money in our training and development activities. | ☐ | ☐ |
> | It is obvious throughout this organization that top management are serious about developing people. | ☐ | ☐ |
>
> ### WHAT ACTION DO YOU NEED TO TAKE?

Indicator 4.5 *The continuing commitment of top management to developing people is communicated to all employees*

This might be viewed as the final logical step in the training and development cycle before, of course, we loop back to the mission/vision and the business plan – and start the process over again.

Having come this far, ensuring that employees continue to recognize the organization's commitment to their development is critical. In practice, this should be seamless with Principle 1. It is basically a matter of keeping the public commitment, made at the outset, fresh in the minds of everyone in the organization.

That is not quite as simple as it might seem. We all know that these things are comparatively easy to start up, and much more difficult to maintain in the face of production pressures, cost reductions, and so on. That is one of the reasons so many quality initiatives fail within the first year or two.

But in order to maintain the business benefits achieved, it is essential to find ways of demonstrating to your employees that your Investors in People endeavours have not been a one-off. That would be particularly damaging if your people have become sceptical due to the introduction

97

of a series of other initiatives that have failed to produce demonstrable benefits.

How to do it

- Ensure that you keep up the commitment, reporting and evaluation systems that you have developed;
- Absolutely vital, ensure that any significant change in business direction, or in training and development policy or practice, is communicated effectively and sensitively;
- Celebrate success. Use whatever media are at your disposal – in-house newsletters, local newspapers, meetings, presentations, memos, notices on the notice boards, and so on;
- Make public the achievements of individuals, teams, and the organization as a whole:
  - a new order won through employee endeavour or efficiency
  - favourable comments received from key customers
  - an individual or group attaining a particular standard, such as a vocational qualification.

Temperature check ✓

	YES	NO
We are good at keeping our people informed about changes in business direction.	☐	☐
Our employees understand that changes in training and development policies/practices are made for good reasons.	☐	☐
Success is celebrated – at organization, team and individual level.	☐	☐
The contribution of training and development to our successes is well publicized.	☐	☐
If an assessor came into our organization today, our employees would tell him or her that our commitment is ongoing.	☐	☐

WHAT ACTION DO YOU NEED TO TAKE?

---

8 Working towards recognition

In earlier chapters, we have examined the business case for Investors in People, looked at how it links with other strands of your approach to total quality, explored the national standard in some detail, and looked at options and recommendations to help you achieve it.

Bearing in mind that the book is based on the four 'As' – awareness, assessment, advice and action – I hope you have been using the 'Temperature checks' to help highlight the areas in which you need to develop as you move towards the standard.

This final chapter takes you through the preparatory and assessment process from beginning to end, to help you put forward a successful case for recognition. It will cover:

- The initial diagnosis, action planning and development work;
- Building your portfolio;
- Using narrative to enhance the portfolio;
- Preparing for assessment, including trial assessment;
- The formal assessment, and how the recognition process works;
- Life beyond recognition.

In outline, the process looks like Figure 22.

Diagnosis, action planning and development

Diagnostic work can take a number of forms. You may already have a fair idea of how good you are at developing your human resources. It can however be a salutary experience to see yourself in the Investors in People mirror.

I find that larger (and sometimes very well known) organizations are somewhat shocked when they find that the systems they thought worked so well, don't. You must, therefore, be able to take an objective

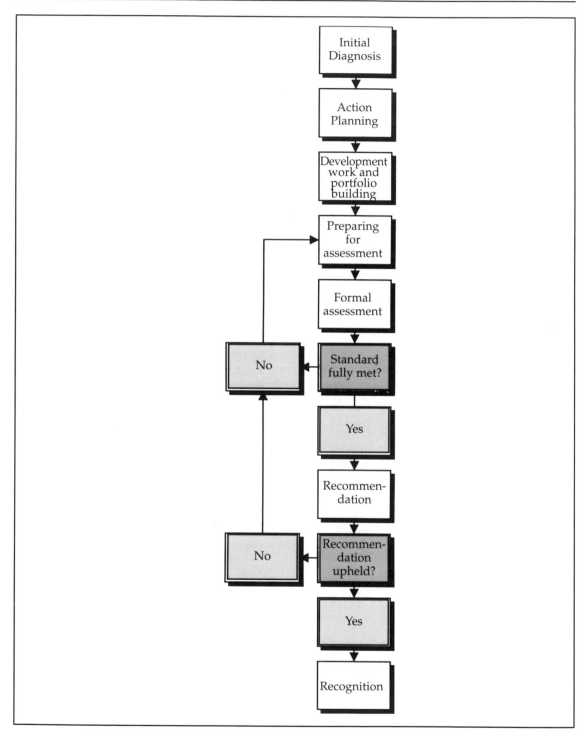

Figure 22   The Investors in People preparation and assessment process in outline

look at your organization's HR policies and practices against the Investors in People standard.

This can be handled in three ways:

1. You can carry out the initial diagnosis yourself.
2. It can be done by a representative of your LEC or TEC.
3. An independent consultant can do it for you.

Doing it yourself

There are advantages and disadvantages to each of these methods. The do-it-yourself method – based on the checklists included in this book, or the diagnostic materials which you can obtain from most of the LECs and TECs – has the advantage of low cost. It can also be a very useful development process for employees involved in it, encouraging ownership and understanding of what good human resource development is all about. The only thing it has against it is possible lack of objectivity and uncertainty as to whether you are going in the right direction, in the absence of an independent view.

Given that you can get advice from your LEC/TEC, the do-it-yourself approach to initial diagnosis is certainly worth considering.

Employee surveys

An employee survey can be a very useful part of the initial diagnosis. This will provide you with some fresh insights into what your people think about the organization and your investment in them. The survey can be repeated later on in the preparatory process to measure progress towards the national standard and, once you have become a recognized Investor in People, it would be worth repeating occasionally, to help make sure your standards are not slipping.

There are a number of formats for an employee survey:

*   You can use the mini-survey introduced in the Introduction (pages 8–10). Remember to modify it to suit your particular needs.
*   You can use a much fuller survey which you have prepared yourself.
*   You can have a consultant do it for you.
*   Investors in People UK and Investors in People Scotland produce a standard format, which is quite comprehensive – but you really do need to adapt it to your situation, as some of the terminology might not fit with your own. The basic survey format is widely available from LECs and TECs.

Using a consultant

If you decide to use a consultant, make sure it is someone with a track record in helping organizations towards recognition. There are many consultants in the human resource development field and they come from a wide variety of backgrounds. A detailed knowledge and understanding of the Investors in People national standard is essential. Take advice from your LEC or TEC on choosing a consultant, although the final decision on who to use will be yours.

Action planning

The initial diagnosis will provide you with a picture of where you will need to develop. The best way of controlling this development work is probably through an action plan, setting out what needs to be done, by when, and by whom.

It is advisable to work back from your target date for recognition or formal assessment, setting dates for the completion of key actions en route.

Action plans can take any number of forms. My favourite version is a Gantt chart, as in the example set out in Figure 23.

It should go without saying that the action plan must be kept under constant review. Specific actions planned and their achievement will form useful topics for meetings with managers and other employees.

Development work

As with the other aspects of the preparation process, much of the development phase can be carried out by you and your employees, with some advice from the LEC/TEC or perhaps from a consultant. The main benefit of involving your people is to give them a deeper insight into the processes and the rationale behind them, thus enriching the preparation and increasing the potential benefits.

Building your portfolio of evidence

The portfolio of evidence is one of the means by which the assessor will be able to form a view of whether you meet the national standard. The other key element of the assessment process is the verbal evidence given by you and your employees. It is worth bearing in mind that the formal

Investors in People Action Plan

Indicator	Specific actions	Responsibility	Target dates for completion (W/C)						
			July	August	September	October	November	December
1.1	Personal letter to all employees	MD/Chair						
1.2	Prepare/issue mission statement	MD/Investors in People steering group						
Etc...								
	Trial assessment	Investors steering group						
	Portfolio completion	Investors steering group						
	Provisional formal assessment	Investors steering group						

Figure 23   Sample Investors in People action plan

103

assessment is based roughly 20–30 per cent on the portfolio and 70–80 per cent on the verbal evidence that should support it.

The portfolio is nonetheless a valuable part of the process because it can help focus your attention, and that of your employees, on the key processes for training and development.

I recommend you start to develop your portfolio as early as possible – once you start to pull together the first 'rough cut', it will help you to identify gaps in your evidence. This is illustrated in Figure 24.

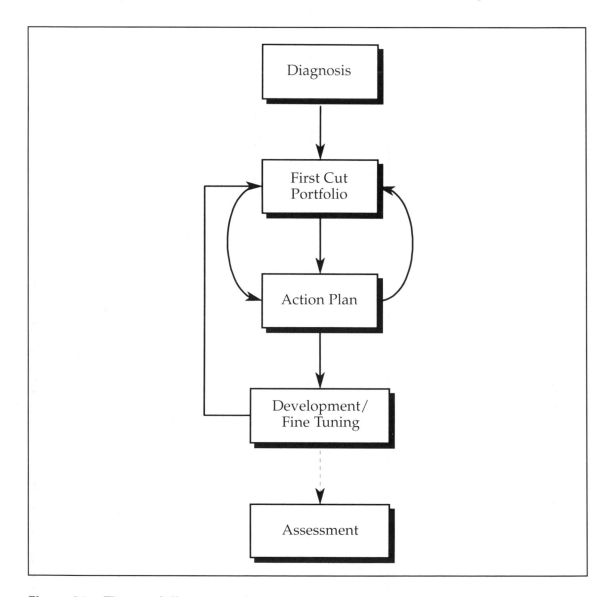

Figure 24   The portfolio as a project management tool

Why develop a portfolio at all?

You may feel that you can put your organization forward for assessment without preparing a portfolio. That may be true – up to a point. Strictly speaking, you could dump all your evidence in a large box and leave it for the assessor to work his or her way through it. But the assessment will probably take longer and may cost you more. Although you could still be recognized even on that basis, it hardly conveys the impression of a quality organization, which given your interest in Investors in People, you will no doubt wish to demonstrate.

'The Portfolio'

Your portfolio does not have to be particularly elaborate. The following hints are based on my experience with a range of organizations, but it is up to you to decide what is best for you. The 'best' portfolios have a logical flow and structure, with the links between the various aspects of the business development and people development processes clearly described.

A well presented portfolio should also give your people that little bit of added confidence when they face the assessor.

Portfolio contents

The following are my recommendations (see Figure 25). But remember, they are not mandatory. They are explained below.

Portfolio Part One

Short statement from the chief executive

This should be brief – say six to eight lines, stating the chief executive's business values, how they feel the development of people keys into this and why recognition as an Investor in People is important. In my portfolio, it would be signed personally by the chief executive.

Contents page

Listing the main sections of the portfolio, giving page numbers and/or document numbers.

Evidence checklist or matrix

Summarizing the documentary evidence contained in the portfolio, and highlighting which indicators they satisfy. The reason for using a checklist/matrix is that one piece of evidence might satisfy more than one indicator. A sample matrix is shown in Figure 26.

Organization chart

This will help the assessor to form a quick picture of the shape of the organization, and also to select a sample of employees for interview. The locations of other branches, depots or plants and the numbers employed at each address will also be helpful.

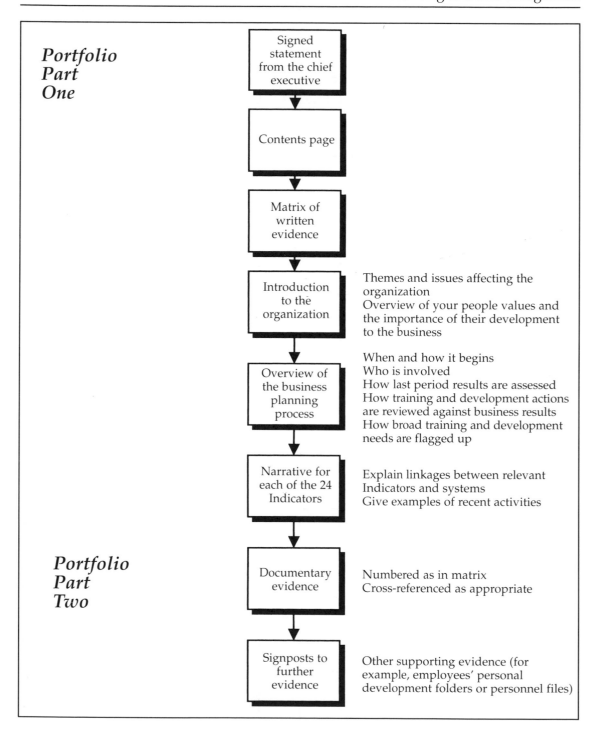

Figure 25   How my portfolio would be constructed

Portfolio Reference	Assessment Indicators																											
	1.1	1.2	1.3	1.4	1.5	1.6	2.1	2.2	2.3	2.4	2.5	2.6	2.7	3.1	3.2	3.3	3.4	3.5	3.6	4.1	4.2	4.3	4.4	4.5			

Figure 26 Investors in People evidence matrix

Introductory narrative

A couple of pages on the organization – who you are, what you do, how, why, and so on. Mission and goals (broadly stated). Main issues facing the company recently, now and in the future – for example contraction or expansion of the business, introduction of quality initiatives, customer care policies, and so on. In other words, setting the scene and context for the development of people in line with achieving your business objectives. Cover the history of the organization briefly if you think it is relevant. Describe in broad terms how your human resource development policies and processes fit with what the business is trying to achieve, and how they contribute to improving the business.

The four Principles and 24 Indicators

My portfolio would contain:

- A narrative describing the processes and how they fit together;
- The documentary evidence itself.

There are various ways of doing this, but the most effective is to state the indicator in full, then make a short statement underneath, saying how you meet it, and how the processes link with other parts of the standard. To some extent, this will repeat your introductory narrative, but it will extend it and help the assessor to understand the processes in relation to the specific requirements of the Indicators. Within the narrative, mention the pieces of evidence you are submitting, and refer to them also by document numbers or some other form of referencing. Some hypothetical examples of portfolio narrative are given below.

Portfolio Part Two

The documents themselves are best filed in a separate binder, in numerical sequence. Remember that the tendency is towards slimmer portfolios – it is generally recognized that one piece of evidence per Indicator, or two if you absolutely must, is sufficient, provided that collectively (and together with the verbal evidence) they tell the story of how you develop your people in line with your business objectives.

When inserting evidence into the portfolio, ask the following of each piece of paper:

- Is it *really* relevant to Investors in People?
- What Indicator does it belong to primarily?
- What other Indicators does it cross refer to?
- Is it surplus to portfolio requirements?

- Is it sufficient for evidence purposes?
- Is it current?

Remember also that you can keep further evidence elsewhere, in files or on computer. If this is the case, signpost it within the portfolio.

Presentation tips

- Ensure that the flow of the narrative and evidence is logical.
- Look for consistency – do the various documents and processes link together?
- Consider whether the process is easy to understand (for a complete stranger).
- Use good quality ring binders – avoid hard-binding your portfolio, as you might want to make amendments right up until the last moment.
- Use two binders. The first should contain all the narrative, and the second the documentary evidence itself. This will make it easier for you – and the assessor – to flick between narrative and evidence.
- Title it prominently – show your pride and confidence in what you are doing in training and development.
- Use section dividers and title pages for the main parts of the portfolio.
- Use flowcharts where you think these will help to explain your approach – for example to show how your business planning process works and where your training and development plans and actions fit into this.
- You might want to mark on each piece of evidence which main Indicator you believe it satisfies (you could add cross references if you like). Do not worry that you might get it wrong. It is the assessor's job to look for all the evidence. What you are doing is helping to make it simpler and easier to follow.

Above all, remember the assessor is coming to help you achieve recognition. There is no such thing as failure. If the assessor does not feel you satisfy all the Indicators, he or she will tell you which ones you need to do further work on, and re-assessment will be based on these alone (unless a major change takes place in your organization in the meantime).

The chances are that if you have prepared thoroughly and have taken good advice where necessary – and most of all if you are serious about developing your people to develop your business – you will be in good shape for recognition. And your business will have benefited from the process.

Using narrative to enhance your portfolio

The following are examples of how narrative might be used to explain how specific Indicators are satisfied, and how the evidence links with that Indicator and with other Indicators. This assumes that there is an introductory narrative to the portfolio, which sets the scene about the organization and its general approach to developing people. The following are examples only. They are based on experience, but are necessarily hypothetical.

Indicator 1.3: *'There is a written but flexible plan which sets out business goals and targets'*

Sample narrative:

Our 1995/6 Operating Plan sets out our objectives for the year, within the context of our three-year strategic plan. Business objectives are set at organization and team levels, and express our priorities of improving customer care, contributions to profit, and our share of the market for servicing and repair of domestic electrical white goods. Our objectives and priorities are summarized for the information of all staff, in a one page extract (document 12) which is updated and re-issued to all staff at least every six months.

The plan is reviewed formally every three months, by discussion at board level and also taking into account views expressed at staff meetings. The plan acts as the focus for all our training and development activities, through individual job descriptions (Indicator 1.5) and the annual review of training needs at individual level (Indicator 2.3).

Indicator 2.6: *'Targets and standards are set for development actions'*

Sample narrative:

It is the responsibility of all managers to ensure that the training and development activities agreed with their staff relate to the achievement of our business objectives. Managers are required to discuss the learning objectives of the proposed training/ development event and their relevance to business objectives with the individual, before the event takes place. These are recorded in the Training and Development Request Form (document 18). Where possible, specific standards of performance are agreed, which the learner will aim to achieve on completion of the training/ development activity. These are, in the main, based on improvements in production and quality, such as individual output or rejection rates. In some cases, the standards set within recognized Vocational Qualifications are adopted (see Indicator 2.7).

The setting of objectives and standards allows managers and staff to evaluate the effectiveness of training/development activities (see Indicators 4.2 and 4.3).

Indicator 3.6: *'Managers are actively involved in supporting employees to meet their training and development needs'*

Sample narrative:

Managers' job descriptions (document 8) specify their responsibilities for supporting the training/development activities of their staff. This is also set out in the Training Policy (document 4). In order to facilitate this process, all managers have been trained in coaching, staff appraisal and counselling, in line with Indicator 2.5. The way in which managers support their staff in training/development is monitored as part of the evaluation procedures set out in the Training Policy (document 4).

Indicator 4.4: *'Top management understand the broad costs and benefits of developing people'*

Sample narrative:

Training and development activities, broad costs and achievements are a standing agenda item at monthly board meetings and also at weekly management/staff meetings (document 22 – agenda for board meetings 17 March 1995 and 21 April 1995, and document 23 – minutes of senior managers' meeting 25 April 1995). The minutes of board meetings are commercial in confidence but can be viewed by the assessor on request.

In addition, all requests for training and development activities must be authorized by a director or senior manager, who is responsible for seeing that the request is in line with business objectives and offers the most cost-effective approach to the need identified. Managers are required to report on training authorized, at the weekly senior managers' meetings.

Preparing for assessment

The months leading up to the formal assessment are of course the time to make final adjustments to your systems and to ensure that communications with your employees are maintained.

This brings us to the question of trial assessment, about which there are two schools of thought. Some people feel that a trial assessment is a waste of time and money, because it is similar to the formal process that will follow shortly. Others feel that it is pointless to go forward for formal assessment without testing the ground first. Whether you have a trial assessment or not is largely up to you, although some LECs and TECs insist on it before they will support your application for a formal assessment.

The answer may depend on how you view the formal assessment. Is it something that you feel you have to get through first time? Or do you see it as a learning experience in itself? How will your workforce feel if you do not make it through? Are they so psyched up about it that 'failure' will demotivate them? Most organizations I have worked with want to get through the formal assessment first time, and are inclined towards having a trial assessment to help them with their final preparation.

I used to hold the view that the trial assessment and the formal assessment are almost identical. Experience has shown me that, although there are some similarities, they are in fact quite different. The trial assessment tends to be considerably more relaxed and informal, with advice and feedback given as it proceeds – all this taking place in the knowledge that 'well, it is only a trial – we've got some time left to finalize things before the real assessor comes along'. The formal assessment tends to be more structured, with virtually no feedback given until the end. So they are, in reality, two different animals and require to be approached differently.

As you know, 70–80 per cent of the assessment is based on discussions with employees, with the remainder based on the portfolio. The assessment process can be quite stressful for some people. They may not be sure what the assessor is looking for, they may be worried about saying the 'wrong thing' and letting the organization down. So it is very important to try to settle your people immediately before the assessment by, for example:

● Briefing them on what is involved and the sort of questions they might be asked – some likely questions are given below;
● Helping them to understand how their comments will be taken into account in the overall context of the assessment – the assessor is unlikely to put much store in a few negative or lukewarm

113

'Right then, who wants to speak to the nice assessor?'

comments. If they are a recurring feature of the assessment, that will be a different matter;
- Emphasizing that it is an assessment of the organization, not of individuals;
- Reassuring them that it is confidential – the assessor will not feed back individual comments;
- Letting them see the portfolio, so that they can refer confidently to documents and systems as appropriate (they are not expected to know these in detail. They do not have to be training experts!).

The formal assessment

The assessor's job is to:

- Ensure that your organization meets all the Indicators;
- Satisfy him or herself that systems, however informal, are in place – and that they work in practice;

114

- Establish whether people agree that the systems work for them as individuals;
- Find the evidence to support this.

The assessment consist of two elements:

1. Examination of your written evidence – the portfolio and perhaps some supporting documents – which will account for roughly 20–30 per cent of the assessment.
2. Discussions with employees.

A week or two before the dates agreed for the formal assessment, the assessor will contact you – and may visit you – to check details, including your eligibility to be assessed as an independent organization, discuss arrangements for the assessment, get advance access to your portfolio, and perhaps meet some of the key people in your organization. This is not part of the formal assessment. It is simply a sensible way of getting the assessment off on the right footing.

The assessor will discuss with you the numbers and types of people he or she wants to talk to. The selection will be at the assessor's discretion, but your advice will be taken into account in gaining access to people in remote locations, and so on.

Getting to a cross section of the workforce

The assessor will want to talk to a cross section of people from different parts of the workforce. How the sample is selected will depend on the size and structure of the organization, but the assessor will want to ensure that the sample group is representative in terms of:

- Physical location;
- Type of job;
- Position/level in the organization;
- Shift workers, job sharers, part-time and casual workers.
- Age, gender, and ethnic mix;
- Disabled people;
- Length of service.

Within this general framework, the assessor will be interested in talking to:

- People who have recently changed jobs within the organization, including those who have been promoted;
- Sub-contractors whose work is part of your core business;

- Employee representatives, if you have them (with reference to Indicator 1.6).

It is worth emphasizing a number of key aspects of the formal assessment process:

- The assessor is there to help you to get recognition.
- It is the assessor's job to help you put forward your case – if there is a gap in your evidence, the assessor will ask you to explain and to provide the evidence that seems to be missing. They are not there to 'fail' you.
- The assessor will be looking for 'naturally occurring' evidence – that is, systems that exist for the good of the business and the people in it, not developed specially for the assessment. Of course, preparation for Investors in People might have caused you to create new systems or modify those already in existence, and these will normally have to be bedded in before you go forward to the formal assessment stage. But that is quite different from cobbling something together just to get through the assessment. Investors in People assessors are adept at detecting the 'smell of fresh paint'.
- This is not an assessment of individuals – it is an assessment of the organization. Make sure your people know that.
- If satisfied that you meet the standard, the assessor will be taking your case to the recognition panel – acting, in effect, as your advocate. The assessor will be required to demonstrate that the assessment has been carried out with due rigour. Before they can do that, he or she will need to be quite satisfied that your case is sound.
- If you do not meet the standard in full, the assessor will tell you where the gaps lie, and will refer you back to the LEC or TEC for further advice. In order to maintain objectivity, the assessor cannot advise you on how to fill the gaps – that is for you and your advisors to decide.
- Re-assessment can take place as soon as you feel ready, subject to the agreement of the LEC or TEC, and is normally only concerned with those areas where you did not meet the standard at the earlier assessment.

Likely areas for discussion

Your employees might appreciate a little advance preparation in terms of having some idea of the questions they will be asked, and how they might answer them. I have often found employees (particularly managers) somewhat diffident in answering these questions, because they are not sure what is 'right' and 'wrong', or because they are a bit vague on the detail or terminology. Usually, the answers are in there somewhere, but may take a lot of digging to bring to the surface.

Here are the sorts of questions/topics that are likely to come up.

Directors and managers

What are the organization's goals and targets for the current year?
What is the business planning cycle, how are people involved in it?
How are business objectives communicated to employees?
What broad training and development needs flow from these – are they set out in the business plan?
How were these arrived at?
How, broadly, is the organization dealing with these needs?
What budget has been allocated for training and development for the current year?
How was this figure arrived at – how does this translate in terms of your department/area/branch?
What other resources are committed?
How do you know you are getting business benefits from this commitment – what actual results can you quote?
How is your training and development activity planned?
How does your training and development activity link with your business goals – how do you move from broad needs to specifics?
How often are business objectives reviewed?
How often is training and development reviewed against the business plan/objectives?
In what way are you personally involved in:
- Reviewing training and development against the business objectives?
- Helping your staff to identify and meet their training and development needs?
- Supporting your staff in their learning?
- Evaluating the results of training and development activities?
Who else contributes to these processes?
How did you develop your own competences in training and developing your team?
How does the organization's evaluation of training and development activities inform its further development plans?

Although the above points relate mainly to the current business planning cycle, you must be able to describe the full training/development loop. If your current business plan is less than a few months into its cycle, you may need to refer to results achieved against earlier plans.

117

Other staff

Describe the future direction/vision/goals of the company.

How are you expected to contribute to these – how do you know?

How often are you brought up to date on the organization's plans, and what they mean for your development?

How do you hear about important changes to the business objectives?

How often are your training and development needs reviewed?

How is this done?

Who is responsible for your training and development?

In what ways does your manager help you in your training and development?

How are targets/standards set for training and development actions?

How do you and your manager know whether training/ development actions have been effective?

When did you last have any training or development?

What targets and standards were agreed?

How did it help you in your job – how do you know?

What help did your manager give you in applying what you learned to your job?

How does top management demonstrate its ongoing commitment to developing you?

Two additional points to bear in mind:

- It can be helpful for managers and staff to refer to written evidence in the portfolio, in support of their responses – it lets the assessor see that the systems work in practice;
- Encourage employees to put forward anecdotal evidence based on their recent experience – quoting from real life experience can go a long way to show that it works at the individual level. Guide them to think through the following statements and attempt to complete them:

    Our business plan required . . .

    So, at my six monthly individual training/development review, my manager and I agreed that I should learn to . . .

    We agreed a target/standard of . . .

    I then attended a half-day seminar on the subject of . . .

    When I came back, my manager and I discussed the results of the training and what further help I needed to achieve the target/standard . . .

    About a month after the training, I found I was able to . . .

    And this led to (benefits to the organization)

Recognition at last

Congratulations – and A Word of Caution

You have managed to impress the assessor with the standard of your approach to developing people, and your case has been upheld by the recognition panel. Congratulations on being recognized as an Investor in People!

Be careful to ensure that the final recognition does not come across as an anti-climax. The run up – from trial assessment, through final

'Aw shucks, it was nuthin.'

preparation and formal assessment to presentation to the recognition panel – will have taken weeks or possibly months. Your people will have been mentally prepared for the trial assessment and probably even more keyed up for the formal assessment. Even when the assessor tells you that he or she is putting you forward to the panel, there can still be an anti-climax when recognition is announced. So keep encouraging your people, and make sure your recognition is seen as a cause for celebration. It is their success.

Life after recognition

It is a condition of recognition that your organization is re-assessed every three years, or if a major change occurs in its structure or ownership.

It is recommended that you undertake an internal management review at least once a year. Of course, I agree with this. But I would remind you that the whole point of Investors in People is to improve your business. It is a process of continuous improvement and in my view should be constantly monitored. I strongly recommend that you put in place a system for ongoing review, covering:

- Continuing review of your systems for identifying and meeting training and development needs;
- Continuing dialogue at meetings, and through your other communications channels, on training and development – this includes formal representative structures where they exist (as required by Indicator 1.6);
- Constant reinforcement that top management are committed to the development of their people;
- Looking for opportunities to recognize and celebrate the success of individuals, teams or the organization as a whole;
- Ensuring that the people dimension figures prominently in all aspects of your business – and particularly that Investors in People is linked to all other quality and business development initiatives you plan to undertake.

Now that you have it, you must live up to it! Anything less could switch your people off for good.

Bibliography

The following list has been compiled on the basis of practicality, readability and relevance to the subject of developing people in line with business objectives. The titles listed offer a mix of practical and academic approaches and should appeal to HR professionals and managers except where stated otherwise.

Coates, Jonathan (1994), *Managing Upwards,* **Aldershot: Gower**

A highly enjoyable slim hardback (95 pages), easy to read, with a clear layout and style. Defines managing upwards, and discusses why it is desirable. It goes on to describe how managing upwards can add to the potential of the organization, and what managers really manage. Gives advice on making it happen, and the skills involved. Useful examples and references to acknowledged experts in the field. Some good visuals.
This book has a wide appeal and key messages for all organizations.

Hunter, Dale, Bailey, Ann, and Taylor, Bill (1992), *The Zen of Groups – a Handbook for People Meeting with a Purpose,* **Aldershot: Gower**

Very good, practical hardback of around 196 pages. Easy to read, with a light, open structure which is not at all daunting. Deals with groups in a broad sense, from work groups through family to community and recreational groups. Deals with the nature of groups, how they work, group development, people in groups, guidelines for facilitators, and achieving synergy. Presents 'meeting models' for various group situations. There are numerous prompts and checklists throughout the book. There are also 95 activities for improving the effectiveness of groupwork.
Would appeal to anyone faced with the task of getting results through groupwork.

Industrial Society, the (1993), *Management Skills – a Practical Handbook,* **London: The Industrial Society**

> This 490 page paperback is very practical with an open structure which makes it easy to dip in to. It is based on the manager as leader, and the managers' responsibility for communicating with the team. It covers a range of important management topics such as selection, induction, appraisal, target setting, training, motivation, delegation, discipline, briefing and managing for total quality. John Adair's Action Centred Leadership model – achieving a balance of emphasis on the Task, the Team and the Individual – is developed into a framework for leadership. There are a number of useful checklists and some brief references to traditional 'motivationalists' such as Maslow, Herzberg and McGregor.
>   Applicable to virtually all levels of manager.

Kirby, Andy (1992), *Games for Trainers (volumes 1, 2, 3),* **Aldershot: Gower**

> These are exactly what they say – games for trainers. Three volumes, ranging from 160–200 pages, in hardback. Each volume contains a wide range of games from ice-breakers and energisers to issue-specific activities such as those on gender and equal opportunities issues. Objectives and instructions are given, together with ideas for modifications to suit particular purposes.
>   For the trainer or manager who needs something to deal with the 'blank stare' syndrome when running in-house group development activities. So get out your card, scissors, glue and string for some fun with a serious intent. Excellent books, practical and easy to understand.

Stimson, Nancy (1991), *How to Write and Prepare Training Materials,* **London: Kogan Page**

> Informal and very practical, this 170 page hardback will be of benefit to professional trainers as well as busy managers who have to run occasional training sessions. Offers hints and tips on preparing training materials, with exercises and checklists to re-inforce the points made. Each chapter has a useful summary at the beginning.

Beardwell, Ian and Holden, Len (1994), *Human Resource Management,* **London: Pitman**

> This 'blockbuster' of 680 pages is essentially a collection of papers from a wide range of contributors. It is very comprehensive, dealing with topics right across the human resource management and development

spectrum. Main sections deal with human resources in its organizational context, resourcing the organization, developing the human resource, the employment relationship and international perspectives on HR. Some excellent visual material and good case studies.

A good one for HR professionals to have on their bookshelves, to consult when necessary.

Thomson, Rosemary and Mabey, Christopher (1994), *Developing Human Resources,* **Oxford: Butterworth-Heinemann**

A quite densely packed hardback of 240 pages, enlivened by case studies, visuals, examples and self-development activities. Examines such topics as developing HR for the 21st century, devising HR strategies and putting them into practice, auditing HR, developing motivation and commitment, assessing and appraising performance, managing organization development and change, and so on.

Should appeal to a wide range of managers and HR professionals.

Moorby, Ed (1991), *How to Succeed in Employee Development,* **Maidenhead: McGraw-Hill**

180 page hardback, which should appeal to managers and HR professionals alike. Deals with the practicalities and politics of employee development, mission, vision, strategy, policies and plans. Goes on to look at identifying training needs, making a financial case for training, options for implementation and so on. Very helpful on linking employee development to business strategy and gives an interesting insight into the author's vision of employee development in the future. Has a pleasant open format.

Megginson, David, Matthews, Jennifer Joy, and Banfield Paul (1993), *Human Resource Development,* **London: Kogan Page (in collaboration with the Association for Management Development)**

A 160 page hardback which should have wide appeal. It has a lively approach enhanced by visuals, questions to consider and checklists. Examines among other things basic issues and current leading ideas in HRD, looks at the learning process and how to manage it, managing learning and change through groups, and world-class HRD.

Pepper, Allan D (1984/92), *Managing the Training and Development Function,*
Aldershot: Gower

This 290 page hardback is presented in two parts. Part 1 deals with the management of training, and Part 2 discusses manpower development. The book usefully teases out the definitions of *training* and *development* with a detailed treatment of both. It covers, *inter alia*, policies and practices, training opportunities, evaluation, cost/benefit analysis, training as an agent of change, managers as learners and 'teachers', and manpower and organization development.

This is for the HR professional rather than line managers. It uses some good examples, but is low on visual content.

The following titles are also useful and relevant to Investors in People

Forsyth, Patrick (1992), *Running an Effective Training Session*, Aldershot: Gower

MacKay, Ian (1993), *35 Checklists for Human Resource Management*, Aldershot: Gower

Rae, Leslie (1992), *Guide to In-Company Training Methods*, Aldershot: Gower

Rodwell, John (1994), *Participative Training Skills*, Aldershot: Gower

Woodcock, Mike and Francis, Dave (1994), *Teambuilding Strategy*, Aldershot: Gower

Basadur, Min (1995), *The Power of Innovation*, London: Pitman

Pedler, Mike, Burgoyne, John and Boydell, Tom (1991), *The Learning Company*, Maidenhead: McGraw-Hill

Buckley, Roger and Capel, Jim (1990), *The Theory and Practice of Training*, London: Kogan Page

Armstrong, Michael (1992), *Human Resource Management – Strategy and Action*, London: Kogan Page

Index